M000122210

United States Reconstruction across the Americas

Frontiers of the American South

UNIVERSITY PRESS OF FLORIDA

Florida A&M University, Tallahassee
Florida Atlantic University, Boca Raton
Florida Gulf Coast University, Ft. Myers
Florida International University, Miami
Florida State University, Tallahassee
New College of Florida, Sarasota
University of Central Florida, Orlando
University of Florida, Gainesville
University of North Florida, Jacksonville
University of South Florida, Tampa
University of West Florida, Pensacola

United States Reconstruction across the Americas

Edited by William A. Link

University Press of Florida
Gainesville · Tallahassee · Tampa · Boca Raton
Pensacola · Orlando · Miami · Jacksonville · Ft. Myers · Sarasota

NOT FOR RESALE
REVIEW COPY ONLY

Copyright 2019 by William A. Link
All rights reserved
Published in the United States of America.

This book may be available in an electronic edition.

24 23 22 21 20 19 6 5 4 3 2 1

Library of Congress Cataloging-in-Publication Data
Names: Link, William A., editor.
Title: United States reconstruction across the Americas / edited by William A. Link.
Other titles: Frontiers of the American South.
Description: Gainesville : University Press of Florida, 2019. | Series: Frontiers of the American South | Includes bibliographical references and index.
Identifiers: LCCN 2018047488 | ISBN 9780813056418 (cloth : alk. paper)
Subjects: LCSH: Reconstruction (U.S. history, 1865–1877) | Slavery—America—History. | America—History. | United States—History.
Classification: LCC E668 .U97 2019 | DDC 973.8—dc23
LC record available at https://lccn.loc.gov/2018047488

The University Press of Florida is the scholarly publishing agency for the State University System of Florida, comprising Florida A&M University, Florida Atlantic University, Florida Gulf Coast University, Florida International University, Florida State University, New College of Florida, University of Central Florida, University of Florida, University of North Florida, University of South Florida, and University of West Florida.

University Press of Florida
2046 NE Waldo Road
Suite 2100
Gainesville, FL 32609
http://upress.ufl.edu

Contents

List of Illustrations vii

Preface ix

Introduction 1
William A. Link

1. The Legacies of the Second Slavery: The Cotton and Coffee Economies of the United States and Brazil during the Reconstruction Era, 1865–1904 11
Rafael Marquese

2. Reconstruction and Anti-imperialism: The United States and Mexico 47
Don H. Doyle

3. Jamaica's Morant Bay Rebellion and the Making of Radical Reconstruction 81
Edward B. Rugemer

List of Contributors 113

Index 115

Illustrations

FIGURES

1. Antonio Ferrigno, *Florada* 30
2. Antonio Ferrigno, *Colheita* 31
3. Antonio Ferrigno, *Lavadouro* 33
4. Antonio Ferrigno, *O terreiro* 33
5. Antonio Ferrigno, *Ensacamento do café* 34
6. Antonio Ferrigno, *Café para a estação* 36
7. Execution of Maximilian and Mexican generals Mejía and Miramón, *Harper's Weekly* 72

TABLE

1. U.S. and Brazilian coffee markets, 1871–1905 22

Preface

United States Reconstruction across the Americas is the first volume in the Frontiers of the American South series, inaugurated with the first Richard J. Milbauer Lectures on the American South, which occurred in March 2017 at the University of Florida. Our purpose is to explore topics that push our understanding of what makes—and has made—the American South. Further, Frontiers of the American South asks historians to consider different thematic approaches that might provide new views about the historical meaning of the South, how it evolved over time, and the relevance of this evolution for our own time.

Meredith Babb and Sian Hunter have been a part of this series since its inception and have provided indispensable assistance in helping us navigate book publishing. Both Meredith and Sian are exceptional editors, and we have greatly benefited from their skill.

The preparation of this volume involved efforts by a variety of people. First and foremost, I must thank Don H. Doyle, who helped to conceive and organize this volume. Rafael Marquese was a model of patience and fortitude in traveling from his Brazilian home to Gainesville, as was Ed Rugemer in traveling from New Haven to warmer climes southward. Each has been a model of professionalism and timeliness and has contributed to a synergy that resulted in this volume.

I benefited greatly from the assistance of my graduate assistant, Aurelia Aubert, who organized logistics and details effortlessly. Other University of Florida graduate students helped out, including Meagan Frenzer, Lauren Kimbell, and David Meltsner.

Introduction

WILLIAM A. LINK

In *Black Reconstruction* (1935), W.E.B. Du Bois declared that his purpose was to show how "the real hero and center of human interest" during Reconstruction was "the slave who is being emancipated." If emancipated slaves were the "chief witness[es] in Reconstruction," he wrote, they had been "almost barred from court." The African American written record was either destroyed or ignored by historians—especially historians of the early twentieth century describing Reconstruction as a failure that resulted from what they described as "black incapacity." Du Bois disagreed vehemently. Every effort, he wrote, had been made by these historians of Reconstruction to reduce black participation "with silence and contempt." The prevalent understanding of the Civil War and its aftermath meant that "we have got to the place where we cannot use our experiences during and after the Civil War for the uplift and enlightenment of mankind." In the "magnificent drama" of human history, no story was more compelling, Du Bois wrote, than the transportation of ten million Africans into the New World—how they "descended into Hell; and in the third century they arose from the dead, in the finest effort to achieve democracy for the working millions this world had ever seen." That truth had been obscured, Du Bois wrote, because of those who "would compromise with the truth in the past in order to make peace in the present and guide policy in the future."[1]

Du Bois's rendition reflects the contested nature of Reconstruction—in 1935 and today—and how central it remains to understanding American history. But what was Reconstruction, exactly? Freedom for four million enslaved people defined, at a basic level, its revolutionary implications, but Reconstruction also involved many elements central to American life. Put simply, Reconstruction involved, among other things, struggles about what defined the American nation, what citizenship meant, and how and to what extent relations between law and government existed across national, state, and local levels. Reconstruction coincided with the emergence of two further important developments: the triumph of an industrial order and the early development of the United States as a global economic and, to some extent, military power.

Understanding Reconstruction must start with how Congress reshaped the nation at the end of the Civil War. The governments established in the defeated Confederacy during the two years after the war reinstalled some of the South's antebellum leadership and reestablished a regime of white supremacy over freed slaves in the Black Codes. In response, in March 1867 the Thirty-Ninth Congress identified the terms under which the defeated South could reunify with the nation. Over the veto of President Andrew Johnson, Congress seized control of post–Civil War reunification, imposed military control over much of the South, and established a new process by which state constitutions were written. These Reconstruction Acts remade the political and constitutional landscape and altered the terms under which Reconstruction would occur. The most important part of the 1867–68 revolution was the enfranchisement of adult African American males, leading to the adoption and ratification of the Fourteenth and Fifteenth Amendments in 1868 and 1870, respectively, and constitutional protections for black citizenship and voting.

For more than a century, historians have examined the meaning of the Civil War and its aftermath, Reconstruction. A vast literature has reflected Americans' perceptions of themselves and what nationhood, citizenship, and international place has meant. Early-twentieth-century historians, most notably William A. Dunning and his followers, portrayed Reconstruction as a mistaken process that disrupted post–Civil War reunification and prematurely empowered freedmen. Beginning in the early 1930s, this Dunningite paradigm—based on obviously racist assumptions—came under attack. Du Bois famously criticized the presumptions of black incapacity—and, implicitly African Americans' responsibility for the failure of Reconstruction—and shifted focus to the destruction of slavery and the emancipation of four million people from it as the centerpiece of a world process.[2] Revisionist scholars, replacing the Dunningite paradigm, generally ignored Du Bois but agreed in their assessment, seeing Reconstruction as benign and even beneficial. In 1988, Eric Foner's magisterial *Reconstruction*—still the best synthesis—established still another paradigm. Foner portrays Reconstruction as a flawed process whose liberation of black people would not reach fuller fruition until the civil rights era.[3]

Since the publication of *Reconstruction* three decades ago, our understanding of the nineteenth century has undergone renewed scrutiny and, as a result, the widening of our understanding of what the post–Civil War era meant. Much of that scholarship has emphasized the global implications of the Civil War in politics, economics, and ideology. Not only was the creation of a new American nation a result of the war, but this creation occurred in concert with a worldwide emergence of modern nationalism. This meant not only stronger nation-states but also weakened ones. Irredentism—the centrifugal power of nationalism—affected empires across the globe, and the breakup of the American Union reflected an assertion of regional particularism that adopted a nationalistic flavor.

Historians have, for several decades, seen slavery and freedom in their international context. Peter Kolchin's invaluable work compares the destruction of U.S. slavery with the end of Russian serfdom. The comparisons are especially apt in the Atlantic world. Eric Foner's *Nothing but Freedom* (1983) outlines in lucid prose how the end of slavery interfaced with the demise of African slavery in Western history. Using comparisons, Foner asserts, "permits us to move beyond 'American exceptionalism' to develop a more sophisticated understanding of the problem of emancipation and its aftermath."[4]

Nonetheless, Foner's *Reconstruction* mostly omits mention, as do even recent assessments, of where the literature might go in a post-Foner paradigm.[5] It is the contention of this volume that Reconstruction, with all its implication for national self-identity, cannot be understood unless we extend our analysis beyond national borders. Emancipation, nationhood and nationalism, and the spread of market capitalism—all central to U.S. Reconstruction—were interwoven with patterns of post–Civil War global political, social, and economic developments. In common, these essays answer these questions: How can an internationalization of Reconstruction—by considering national history as part of a process involving several state actors—enhance our understanding? How did the Civil War reshape the United States' relationship to the world, regionally and internationally? In what respects did international developments affect the South's transition from a slave to a free society?

The three essays brought together here use various approaches, assumptions, and methodology to explore the international implications of Reconstruction. We make no claim that this book is "transnational" history, but we believe that the international contexts of what occurred in the United States are essential. *United States Reconstruction across the Americas*, which includes the essays of the distinguished international scholars Rafael Marquese, Don Doyle, and Edward Rugemer, provides different answers, reflecting the contested nature of how historians are interpreting the end of the Civil War and its implications.

If slavery's demise was central to Reconstruction, how had it changed during the pre-emancipation era? Scholars have, in general, dispensed with the once-common depiction of U.S. slavery as static, eccentric, premodern, and isolated—and, implicitly, removed from global developments. Instead, they have seen the American slave system as intimately interconnected with global forces driving world capitalism. The American South, by 1860, contained the world's largest and most valuable enslaved population, while southern slaveholders, as a group, reaped fortunes in cotton, rice, sugar, and tobacco. Slavery's profits drove exports, trade, and capital benefiting American and global financial centers. Meanwhile, the protection of slavery remained deeply embedded in the U.S. constitutional system and guided how the national government conducted itself at home and abroad.[6]

Slavery's demise and the transformation of the global plantation system are the subject of this volume's first essay. Rafael Marquese compares the impact of emancipation in the United States and Brazil and the transformation of the coffee and cotton economies. Here, the matter of how to periodize Reconstruction emerges. Traditionally, historians have used the twelve years between the Confederate surrender in 1865 and the final withdrawal of federal troops from the South in 1877 to mark the beginning and end of Reconstruction. Marquese, arguing for a wider view, adopts what some historians call a "Long Reconstruction," which encompassed the end of the nineteenth century and the beginning of the twentieth. He argues that "spatial expansion"—the globalized understanding of American history—should be matched by "temporal expansion" into the twentieth century. Marquese is concerned primarily with what he calls a "profound reorganization of the national state and American capitalism that took place between 1870 and 1914" (16) Marquese connects American Reconstruction with larger global processes. An especially crucial concept is Dale Tomich's "Second Slavery," in which Atlantic slavery—including North America and Latin America—underwent, during the first half of the nineteenth century, a transformation in response to the spread of capitalism and the increasing unification of the world economy. For Marquese, the Second Slavery provides a model for understanding both the "integrated trajectory of slavery in Brazil and the United States" (17) and how the coffee and cotton economies of these nations interacted after emancipation.

In both the United States and Brazil, slavery revitalized itself because of plantation economies that became ever more tightly integrated in the world economy. In the U.S. South, cotton drove a rapid economic expansion throughout the country, the physical and demographic expansion of the enslaved population, and an empowered slaveholder class. In Brazil, the production of coffee, a commodity new to the nineteenth century, spurred the expansion of slavery in northeastern Brazil. Emancipation and its aftermath played out differently in the two countries, however. While in the American South slavery was destroyed only through violent struggle, in Brazil this process occurred more slowly.

After American slavery ended, the economies of the two nations became more integrated, but Brazil's planter class consciously avoided the U.S. model of plantation organization and labor. Rather, they reshaped the labor system by using free labor—cheap immigrant labor, primarily from Italy—under the *colonato* system of small shareholders. The coffee economy flourished under this system. "Although distinct from southern sharecropping," Marquese writes, "both strategies tried to solve the same problem: how to recover the high levels of labor exploitation of slavery times in the post-emancipation period" (29). Although the U.S. South expanded cotton production rapidly under sharecropping and tenancy, this system of land tenure and labor was extremely decentralized and differed significantly from the more centralized enslaved work regime it replaced. In contrast, the *colonato* system centralized planter control over labor and production, work discipline, and harvest and processing of coffee beans. Marquese concludes that "the reconfiguration of the North American capitalist order in the Reconstruction era was an essential constituent part of the crisis of the Second Slavery and the passage from empire to republic in Brazil" (39).

This volume's second essay shifts focus to examine the changing nature of American foreign relations that followed the Civil War—especially as a nascent world power emerging during the 1860s. While Marquese suggests that Reconstruction should be seen as part of global processes of economic change and nationhood, Don Doyle examines what he calls the "international context of America's Reconstruction era" (47), especially in Latin America, that followed in the wake of Union victory in 1865. Rather than seeing Reconstruction as an isolated process, Doyle, using the case study of Mexico, suggests that Reconstruction should be understood globally. In contrast to other historians, who often explain this period as an early manifestation of American imperialism, Doyle argues that Secretary of State William Seward pursued a defensive policy designed to force the withdrawal of European interventions from the Western Hemisphere.

In 1823, President James Monroe, in his annual message to Congress, announced a new policy that opposed further European intervention and colonization in the Western Hemisphere. This new policy, which came to be known as the Monroe Doctrine, became a cornerstone of American foreign policy, but it mostly existed as an abstraction, unenforced by sustained U.S. diplomacy or military power. According to Doyle, Seward made the Monroe Doctrine a "central pillar of postwar U.S. foreign policy" (57). Rather than an instrument of American imperialism, according to Doyle, the Monroe Doctrine appealed to Latin American republicans eager to shed European domination and adopt the ideology of the victorious Union.

In 1867, while the Congress took charge of Reconstruction, Europeans withdrew from the Western Hemisphere. Seward chiefly sought to consolidate the United States' hemispheric position by persuading, through diplomacy and military pressure, Europeans to decolonize its presence. His signature foreign-policy achievement, the purchase of Alaska from Russia in the spring of 1867, reflected this policy of decolonization, according to Doyle, and contributed to Britain's establishment, in the same year, of the Dominion of Canada and a withdrawal of its colonial presence in North America.

During the Civil War, Europeans had seen an opening to expand and even intervene in Latin America. In 1861, while Mexico's northern neighbor was distracted, a combined Anglo-Spanish-French force invaded, but eventually only the remaining French established, in 1864, a new empire under Maximilian I. During the same year, the Spanish occupied the Dominican Republic—independent for only seventeen years—in an attempt to reestablish a Spanish empire in the Caribbean. Not only was the new Mexican Empire the result of a foreign invasion, but it enjoyed the support and participation of anti-republican forces inside Mexico. Maximilian's regime represented, to Americans and Mexicans, an extension of the same concepts underlying the Confederacy.

Not accidentally, when the war ended the Maximilian regime harbored and even sponsored about two thousand Confederate exiles in the northern part of the country. At the same time, about three thousand Union veterans—including the American Legion of Honor—entered Mexico in support of republican forces, while U.S. Army forces fortified the border and supplied rebels with arms. In the end, as a result of U.S. diplomacy and a looming military threat, the French withdrew their forces, the empire collapsed, and Maximilian was executed on June 19, 1867.

The demise of France's Mexican intervention reflected, Doyle maintains, a triumph of cross-national republicanism and, implicitly, a reflection of the international implications of Radical Reconstruction. There was little question, on the one hand, that Americans like Seward feared the "darker" races of Latin America, and that these fears were fueled by racism. At the same time, Seward was motivated by a common sense of republicanism. Through diplomacy and military pressure, Seward eliminated a possible Confederate revival and hostile European presence in Mexico. Rather than an aggressive act of expansion, argues Doyle, U.S. policy reflected a "spirit of republican camaraderie" (72) that coincided with Reconstruction—and ended once Reconstruction ended.

In this volume's final essay, Edward Rugemer reconsiders the Morant Bay Rebellion, an uprising that occurred in October 1865—only six months after the Confederate surrender—that shook the racial hierarchy in Jamaica. The British had instituted emancipation more than thirty years before the rebellion, but the black peasantry remained impoverished and politically disempowered. The rebellion reflected widespread discontent about the contradictions between emancipation and political inequality.

The Morant Bay Rebellion reflected tensions in post-emancipation Atlantic societies, but it was also related to Reconstruction and the ways in which its advocates envisioned the status of freed slaves. In particular, the rebellion provides an example of the dangers of emancipation without political rights. Using the theoretical model of Jürgen Habermas, Rugemer examines how the transition from "opinion formation" to "will formation" shaped the way in which political elites reached decisions. Opinion formation is contested and sometimes chaotic, whereas will formation follows the coalescence of opinion around a policy solution. During the early postwar years, according to Rugemer, the "central political questions . . . revolved around federal policy toward the former Confederate states," but this policy depended on determining former slaves' political and economic status. The decisive turn toward federal intervention during the Thirty-Ninth Congress in 1867—the imposition of "radical" reconstruction—marked the will formation among northern Republican leaders. Opinion formation flowed from public discussion and especially the media of print journalism. What newspapers and political leaders saw and discussed occurring in the postwar South—and in the larger Atlantic world—alarmed them. Opinion leaders did not have to look far in other post-emancipation societies to see an example of emancipation gone off the rails. Rugemer therefore urges historians to examine the "entangled public spheres" of discourse across the Atlantic "that recognizes both the distinctions of political context and the cumulative dimension of slavery's demise" (82–83).

The will formation of Radical Reconstruction—congressional Republicans' decision to intervene in the spring of 1867—reflected these tendencies. The Morant Bay Rebellion exemplified how emancipation and the continued oppression of former slaves in Jamaica could lead to social chaos. The British abolition of slavery still provided for restrictions on the economic and political status of emancipated slaves. This was "nothing but freedom," as a contemporary southerner put it. Former slaves were bound to former masters by laws requiring that they work without pay for a specified period of time—either four or six years—in exchange for rations and housing. They also lacked citizenship or political rights. Emancipated Jamaicans became an oppressed peasantry with little hope for improved status. The Morant Bay Rebellion arose from these conditions, with severe consequences. Rebels killed twenty-two and torched five buildings, but the British response was harsh. Jamaican peasants' villages were burned and 600 flogged, and military courts condemned 354 rebels to hanging.

The Morant Bay Rebellion appeared prominently in the American press. While white southerners feared that these events portended insurrection and mayhem, African American and northern Republican newspapers drew a different conclusion. The rebellion resulted from cruelty and oppression, as well as the lack of a policy accommodating the transition from slavery to freedom. In the immediate aftermath of the destruction of slavery in the Confederate South, Rugemer concludes, the "deeply woven history of Atlantic emancipation" shaped events (99). Newspaper opinion affected congressional opinion, according to Rugemer. He described the evolution of the thinking of the Radical Republican Charles Sumner, who used the example of the "terrible tragedy" in Jamaica as an instructive example of the consequences of injustice to former slaves. Insurrection and political chaos flowed from the "denial of rights to colored people," declared Sumner in 1866, and four million emancipated might be also drawn to a "terrible war of races" without political and economic power (102).

Rugemer suggests in his essay, in other words, that emancipation in the United States must be understood as a global process that was connected to emancipations in other societies ending racial slavery. What occurred in the United States in the adoption of measures such as the Civil Rights Act of 1866, the provision of birthright citizenship in the Fourteenth Amendment, and the enfranchisement of male citizens in the Fifteenth Amendment reflected the "integrated worlds of slavery created by the empires of the eighteenth century." "Black emancipation," writes Rugemer, "was an Atlantic process that was slow, uneven, and interconnected" (106).

This volume's essays offer divergent visions of how we might internationalize Reconstruction by providing a variety of global contexts in which we might understand post–Civil War American history. The essays differ according to subject and method. Rafael Marquese examines new cross-national patterns of labor and economic development; his approach is macro-level economic and social history, and it sets Reconstruction in the context of world events. In contrast, Don Doyle, using the lens of foreign relations, looks at how national developments—the rising rhetoric of international republicanism—shaped American policy through a revitalization of the Monroe Doctrine. Finally, Edward Rugemer draws out still another global context by examining the intersection of public discourse with political processes, showing how discourse crossed borders, from Jamaica to the U.S. Congress, to shape opinion formation and policy making.

These essays are not meant to be final word about the international web of events shaping Reconstruction. Nor are they intended to dismiss the long-held narrative about how and why Reconstruction occurred and with what consequences. Rather, by providing another way to examine this narrative, they are suggestive of new insights that might result from understanding the aftermath—and ultimately the legacy—of the American Civil War in an internationalized context.

Notes

1. W.E.B. Du Bois, *Black Reconstruction in America, 1860–1880* (New York: Harcourt, Brace, and Company, 1935), chap. XVII.

2. Du Bois, *Black Reconstruction.*

3. Eric Foner, *Reconstruction: America's Unfinished Revolution* (New York: Harper & Row, 1988).

4. Steven Hahn, "Class and State in Postemancipation Societies: Southern Planters in Comparative Perspective," *American Historical Review* 95, no. 1 (February 1990): 75–98; Peter Kolchin, *Unfree Labor: American Slavery and Russian Serfdom* (Cambridge: Harvard University Press, 1987); Eric Foner, *Nothing but Freedom: Emancipation and Its Legacy* (1983; Baton Rouge: Louisiana State University Press, 2007), 2.

5. Bruce Baker and Brian Kelly, eds., *After Slavery: Race, Labor, and Citizenship in the Reconstruction South* (Gainesville: University Press of Florida, 2013); Thomas J. Brown, *Reconstructions: New Perspectives on the Postbellum United States* (New York: Oxford University Press, 2006); Luke E Harlow, "Introduction: The Future of Reconstruction Studies," *Journal of the Civil War Era* 7, no. 1 (March 2017): 3–6. For a recent work, consult Martha S. Jones, *Birthright Citizens: A History of Race and Rights in Antebellum America* (New York: Cambridge University Press, 2018).

6. Walter Johnson, *River of Dark Dreams: Slavery and Empire in the Cotton Kingdom* (Cambridge: Harvard University Press, 2013); Sven Beckert, *Empire of Cotton: A Global History* (New York: Vintage, 2015); Matthew Karp, *This Vast Southern Empire: Slaveholders and the Helm of American Foreign Policy* (Cambridge: Harvard University Press, 2016); Robert E. Bonner, *Mastering America: Southern Slaveholders and the Crisis of American Nationhood* (Cambridge: Cambridge University Press, 2009).

1

The Legacies of the Second Slavery

The Cotton and Coffee Economies of the United States and Brazil during the Reconstruction Era, 1865–1904

RAFAEL MARQUESE

In 1904 the federal government of the young Republic of Brazil invested a considerable amount of resources to participate in the Louisiana Purchase Exposition, a celebration marking the one-hundredth anniversary of the Purchase, in Saint Louis, Missouri. Visited by nearly twenty million people over a period of seven months, the event stood out from other expositions for its size. Covering an area of 1,270 acres—nearly two square miles—the fair received exhibits from sixty-three different countries. The U.S. federal, state, and county administrations spent $15 million, while the Brazilian government spent almost $600,000, a quarter of which was used for the construction of the pavilion of the country. The architectural investment paid off during and after the exhibition; the Brazilian building was awarded the gold medal of architecture. Made of metal, the structure was subsequently moved to Rio de Janeiro, then capital of Brazil, where for seventy years it formed part of the urban landscape. When the city hosted the Third Pan-American Conference, in 1906, it was renamed Monroe Palace, later serving as the seat for Brazil's Federal Senate.[1]

The Saint Louis fair and other nineteenth-century exhibitions were modeled on the Centennial International Exhibition, held in Philadelphia in 1876, which displayed the technological advances of the industrial world.[2] The celebration of the new American imperial order, an alliance between federal power and industrial capitalism resulting from the Civil War, was one of the unifying elements of all the exhibitions promoted in the United States between 1876 and 1916. Another element was the combination of new theories of racial hierarchy and the projection of American material and national progress. In Saint Louis the discipline of anthropology played a leading role, with the largest exhibition space reserved for the Philippines, recently made a U.S. colony as a result of the Spanish-American War. About two hundred natives of the archipelago were displayed in a visual discourse that articulated U.S. imperial overseas policies to the racial and class hierarchies that prevailed at home. The emphasis on white supremacy that inspired the entire program of universal exhibitions held in North America mirrored the deep class divisions of post–Civil War America.[3]

The expectations of the young Brazilian Republic in engaging with the Saint Louis exposition were more modest. In the beginning of the twentieth century Brazil was the largest coffee exporter in the world, controlling 75 percent of the global supply. The United States, at the same time, had become coffee's largest importer: the country was responsible for almost half of all world market purchases, 80 percent of which were bought in Brazil. However, a basic problem remained in U.S.-Brazil coffee trade. The most popular coffee varieties in the North American market were Moka and Java, commanding 40 percent of retail sales in the country, but the limited volume of production from Yemen and the Dutch East Indies was unable to meet such a large demand. High-quality Brazilian coffee shipped from Santos and Rio de Janeiro, which often left the coffee plantations in the highlands already classified as Moka and Java, entered the United States market identified as originating in the Indian Ocean basin. U.S. consumers, in short, were paying more for a Brazilian product that American coffee trusts deliberately falsified. Coffee producers had to confront more significant challenges as well. Given the dramatic rise of supply in the aftermath of the abolition of slavery in Brazil, average import prices for the commodity plummeted in the New York market between 1895 and 1903, going from just under 15 cents to less than 7 cents per pound.[4]

These were some of the challenges that the Brazilian representation faced at the exposition in Saint Louis. Coffee advertising became an official priority. The São Paulo delegation, responsible for organizing the exhibition, established a strategy to win the growing midwestern market while also raising the value of the Brazilian product vis-à-vis all American consumers. At Saint Louis, organizers displayed coffee cultivation in Brazil, from coffee shrubs to the transportation of green beans to the market. The delegation further advertised the advanced processing machinery used in Brazil, responsible for the final quality of the product. Visitors could enjoy the superiority of Brazilian beans by drinking freshly prepared coffee on the spot.[5] As part of this program, a series of six oil paintings made by the Italian artist Antonio Ferrigno (1863–1940) depicted the Santa Gertrudes coffee plantation, located in Araras, west of São Paulo. The plantation belonged to the powerful planter and banker Eduardo Prates, a leading figure of the São Paulo political and business group that had seized power in Brazil after the proclamation of the republic. At that time, his plantation—regarded as one of the most advanced coffee-growing units in the world—had become an important center for visitors interested in the coffee economy and technology. Photographs of Santa Gertrudes were exhibited at the Agriculture Pavilion in Saint Louis and incorporated into the official catalog of Brazil. The place of Ferrigno's paintings in Saint Louis was even more noble: they occupied the first floor of the Brazilian Pavilion, in a display that increased the power of the visual effects that had been planned for the exhibition. The U.S. press did not fail to record the impact that this visual strategy, combined with the widespread distribution of high-quality coffee, had over the visitors.[6]

The paintings followed a single pattern, all with the same dimensions and formal composition, representing every step of the productive flux and labor process. They portrayed the plants' flowering announcing a voluminous harvest, while the coffee rows were weeded; labor during harvest; the washing and sorting of the cherries harvested as soon as they had reached the plantation headquarters; the drying of the cherries in the immense *terreiros* (drying platforms); the final processing and bagging of the beans through a fully mechanized process; and the transportation of coffee sacks in oxcarts to the train station located just two kilometers from the plantation headquarters. The paintings emphasized the mechanization of the production process, ensuring a high-quality final product while also representing the predominance of white European workers.

Using these images as the point of departure but also as the point of arrival of the analysis, this chapter argues that the seemingly disconnected processes of the abolition of slavery and Reconstruction in the United States, on the one hand, and of the abolition of slavery and the increasing rates of expansion of the Brazilian coffee exports, on the other hand, were structurally related, mutually conditioning each other by means of the asymmetrical relations that both spaces maintained with the restructuring of the late-nineteenth-century capitalist world economy. Indeed, the series on the Santa Gertrudes plantation marked the convergence of three broad processes: the dramatic growth of the Brazilian coffee economy at the turn of the century; the profound change in the economic and social fabric of the post–Civil War United States, which found in the cycle of universal exhibitions inaugurated in 1876 one of its best ideological projections; and the transition from an order based on slavery to one based on free labor in the American hemisphere. Ferrigno's paintings in Saint Louis represented the outcome of larger historical transformations that were unleashed by the American Civil War and Reconstruction and further unified the historical trajectories of Brazil and the United States.

Efforts to internationalize Reconstruction are not new. Examining the implications of black labor within the world capitalist order, W.E.B. Du Bois in *Black Reconstruction* argued that the Civil War and Reconstruction had global implications. In an argument that in many respects anticipated C.L.R. James's and Eric Williams's writings on the Caribbean, Du Bois pointed out how industrial capitalism depended on the large-scale exploitation of enslaved workers in various places. The presence of these workers in the developed industrial order, in turn, was what ultimately "brought civil war in America."[7] In his analysis of Reconstruction, however, Du Bois focused exclusively on national events, thus failing to exploit all the transnational potential contained in his initial suggestion. This nation-based framework of analysis for the post-emancipation United States, which isolated it from a broader context of reference, remained the paradigm until the 1980s, as American historians in general paid little attention to the hemispheric dimensions. One of the main exceptions to this trend came from an intellectual heir of Du Bois. In a short but innovative compilation of essays, Eric Foner demonstrated how emancipation in the French and British Caribbean guided the subsequent process of emancipation in the United States. Particularly inspiring is his analysis of how the genesis of the sharecropping system during Reconstruction was born out of the clashes between planters and freedmen, conflicts that were shaped by how contemporary actors interpreted the history of the post-abolition Caribbean.[8]

The impact of Foner's book, combined with growing attention paid to the comparative history of slavery in the Americas, contributed to an understanding of the U.S. South within a broader historical framework. A good example of this can be found in Kees Gispen's 1990 edited volume, *What Made the South Different?* Bringing together a leading team of comparative historians of the nineteenth-century United States, the book considers a wide range of subjects in order to explore the particularity of the trajectory of the U.S. South in the Western Hemisphere. Of special interest is Steven Hahn's essay, which deals with the same subject that he had explored in a very influential article of 1990.[9]

In these two pieces, Hahn framed the history of Reconstruction based on a comparative method in order to understand the nature of the reconfiguration of the political, social, and economic power of southern planters after the Civil War, as well as within the broader relations between emancipation and the development of capitalist agriculture in the South. By comparing the construction of the national state and the consolidation of the capitalist order in the United States and Brazil, Hahn explored the distinctions in the character, rhythm, and outcome of these processes, distinguishing the peculiar features of each. If the abolition of slavery was a necessary condition for the consolidation of capitalist agriculture, it did not happen in the same way in both places. Depending on the results of conflicts between former masters and slaves, as well as on the nature of the political configuration that emerged from these struggles, the outcomes proved quite different. The sharecropping system in the South was an expression of the relative weakness of the former planter class in the structures of national power that emerged after the Civil War, when they found themselves in a situation of increasing political and economic subordination to northern industrial and financial interests. The opposite happened in Brazil. "In the course of emancipation and nation-building," writes Hahn, "the landed classes throughout Brazil retained their property, control over labor, and local prerogatives. The coffee planters, furthest along the road of capitalist agriculture, also succeeded in using the resources of the state to advance their interests." The failure of southern landed elites to maintain significant influence in the United States led to the growing subordination of southern cotton interests to the economic power of the victors in the Civil War. "In comparative perspective," he concludes, "what stands out in the course of emancipation and unification is the swift and dramatic decline in the fortunes of the Southern planter class."[10]

While the contrast Hahn draws between planters in post-emancipation United States and Brazil is insightful, how he reaches such a conclusion obscures the *relationship* between both outcomes. His comparison treats the U.S. and Brazilian cases as independent, and, as in other such comparisons, this emphasizes the unique character of each. As Jeffrey R. Kerr-Ritchie recently points out, the use of comparative methods as part of efforts to internationalize the history of Reconstruction has most often reinforced the idea of the exceptionality of the U.S. experience. As a result, the relationship between spaces and processes of abolition/post-abolition become relegated to the background.[11]

Considering the limits of historical comparisons is important because of the remarkable strength that transnational and global perspectives have lately shown. This is clear in a number of recent books and edited volumes of essays dealing with the Civil War in more encompassing approaches, with contributions from some of the best historians who have enlarged the analytical framework for the study of the South during the Civil War era.[12] Spatial expansion is accompanied by temporal expansion in approaches to Reconstruction that incorporate the first decades of the twentieth century in order to account for the profound reorganization of the national state and American capitalism that took place between 1870 and 1914.[13]

In an afterword for a recent collection of essays on *The World the Civil War Made*, Steven Hahn notes that in order to cope with the temporal and spatial enlargement of the problem of emancipation and Reconstruction, it seems impossible not to deal with "the wide-ranging and challenging conceptual and empirical work that we still have before us."[14] Indeed, without a solid theoretical framework it will be difficult to move toward a synthesis that illuminates the interrelationships between the South and the world. Hence the relevance of the concept of the "Second Slavery," which has found wide acceptance among scholars of nineteenth-century slavery in Brazil, Cuba, and the United States.[15] Considering its theoretical and methodological foundations, the concept offers interesting new ways to approach the problem of Reconstruction.

In the original formulation of the Second Slavery concept, Dale Tomich noted how a set of historical events and trends during the late eighteenth and early nineteenth centuries, most notably the advent of the Industrial Revolution and the consolidation of British hegemony over the world economy and the interstate system, led to profound reconfigurations of Atlantic slavery. The growing imbalance in the international prices of industrial and agricultural goods, the increase in the demand for tropical commodities such as coffee and sugar that the growing population of workers and middle classes in the urban centers of the North Atlantic consumed, and the search for new raw materials such as cotton all followed the decline of slavery in the British and French Caribbean. These changes acquired a different meaning in the slaveholding U.S. South, Cuba, and Brazil, areas that became the dynamic centers of a massive expansion of slavery to meet the growing global demand for cotton, coffee, and sugar. New World slavery was re-created through an unprecedented political and economic configuration, and its character and systemic meaning were deeply transformed. Further, industrial production in the world market fueled the growth of these emerging slave zones. According to Tomich, "this 'second slavery' developed not as a historical premise of productive capital, but presupposing its existence and as a condition for its reproduction."[16]

Methodologically, as a comparative tool this analysis is substantive instead of formal. Rather than being treated as external and independent to one another, these slave zones are understood as particular moments of a single historical process of long duration, that is, of a single historical structure (the world economy and the interstate system of the nineteenth century) that shapes these slave zones but at the same time is shaped by them. By attending to the multiple mediations between the world political economy and local conditions, this approach to comparative history examines how spatially separated regions have conditioned each other over time in a process that was both unequal and combined. As this process unfolded, it changed at different paces the conditions of reproduction of the whole (the world economy and the interstate system) and its parts (the slave zones and the political units that composed them).[17] Such an analytical perspective allows us to account not only for the integrated trajectory of slavery in Brazil and the United States but also for the destinies of these two countries *after* abolition. An investigation of the legacies of the Second Slavery through this methodological lens allows us to understand the unified but contradictory nature of the reconfiguration of the cotton and coffee economies of the U.S. South and Brazil within global capitalism after the end of slavery.

The U.S. Civil War represented a profound turning point in the historical structure of nineteenth-century Atlantic slavery. In order to understand how this happened and what its subsequent implications were for Reconstruction in its global dimensions, it is necessary to quickly describe two of the main trends of the Second Slavery: the political and economic relations between Brazil and the United States and the character of slave labor exploitation in their coffee and cotton plantations.

The institutional construction of the Second Slavery was part of the creation of new independent, liberal nation-states in the Americas. It also occurred in a global context marked by the ideological forces of antislavery. Until the mid-1830s the political actors of the Empire of Brazil and the United States answered this challenge within the framework of their own political units, as they sought to solidify an internal front for their defense of slavery. With the mounting international attack on slavery following British emancipation in 1838, along with a stronger transnational alliance between British and American abolitionists in the 1840s, the political powers of the Second Slavery demonstrated a growing convergence in their defensive strategy. The key point of the articulation of this "International Proslavery" was to ensure a balance between its component parts in such a way as to prevent antislavery from advancing within their respective political units. The strength that the southern slaveholding interests expressed in maintaining control of the federal government and its foreign policy, added to the particular character of the southern proslavery ideology, made the United States a central reference for the defense of slavery in the Empire of Brazil during the 1840s and 1850s.[18]

When geopolitical alignment of proslavery power occurred, the bonds between the Brazilian and U.S. economies became stronger. The free-trade platform advocated by southern cotton exporters—reaching its climax in the Nullification Crisis—had huge implications for Brazilian coffee exporters. The tariff policy that settled the sectional crisis in the United States in 1833 ended import taxes on a series of foreign goods, including coffee. Given the increase in Brazilian production and the consequent decline of coffee prices after 1823, the average coffee price in New York in the early 1830s was around 10 cents a pound. With the tariffs in force since 1814, import taxes for coffee amounted to 5 cents a pound. The tax-free policy of 1833 therefore led to an automatic decrease of 50 percent in the final value of the coffee that was purchased by the American consumer. With the exception of the period from 1861 to 1872, the importation of tax-free coffee in the United States lasted until the end of the nineteenth century. In less than two decades (1830–50), one in every four sacks of coffee produced in the world would be shipped to American ports.[19]

The consequence of this new tariff policy for the growth of coffee plantations in Brazil was immediate. Americans were not the only consumers of Brazilian coffee, but by 1850 they had indisputably become their main buyers. In the 1830s, on average the United States imported 28 percent of the coffee sent by Brazil to the world market. By the midcentury, when Brazilian coffee growers controlled about 40 percent of total global supply, 43 percent of their exports went to the United States. The Brazilian position in the North American market became a virtual monopoly: 93 percent of the coffee imported by the United States in 1850 came from the port of Rio de Janeiro.[20]

Notwithstanding the exports of wheat flour to Brazil, the trade balance between the two countries remained negative for the United States. Surpluses from the exports of raw cotton to Great Britain more than compensated for the trade deficit with Brazil, however. The characteristics of slave labor in cotton and coffee production in the United States and Brazil during the Second Slavery, solidly established in the 1820s, were maintained with small variations until the outbreak of the Civil War. Southern cotton production grew from 180 million bales in 1820 to 1,390 million in 1860, the equivalent of roughly two-thirds of the world supply; during the same period, Brazil's coffee production went from 12,000 to 180,000 metric tons, almost half of the world's supply. These were very close trajectories of expansion. The massive supply of southern cotton and Brazilian coffee resulted from the spatial mobility of the commodity frontier, the steady incorporation of new slaves, and, most importantly, the intensification of the exploitation of these workers.[21]

It is possible to observe, in this last aspect, another manifestation of the common process that encompassed the two economies. In spite of their agronomic differences, weeding in cotton and coffee plantations was organized in gangs under the unified command of an overseer. In order to satisfy the demand for more exports, the area under cultivation increased steadily from the 1830s. In the U.S. South, the measurement of the ratio of the labor force to the planted area was made by calculating the amount of acres in cotton and corn allocated to each field slave. In more productive regions such as Louisiana's alluvial lands, this proportion reached an impressive rate of twelve acres of cotton and eight acres of corn per slave laborer. In the Brazilian coffee economy the measurement was based on the proportion of coffee shrubs per field slave. Whereas in the eighteenth- and early-nineteenth-century Caribbean this proportion was somewhere between one thousand to two thousand shrubs per slave, by the mid-1850s in the most productive areas of Brazil it had reached the mark of four thousand to five thousand. These increases in the workload on the cotton and coffee plantations meant that more product per hand would have to be collected during the harvest. The management strategy individualized the control of slave labor with a task system based on the imposition of personal quotas that were individually quantified at the end of each day. These quotas sought to adjust the total volume of cotton and coffee to be harvested to the skill, individual capacity, and picking history of each slave. The evaluation of the minimum quotas was combined with a perverse system of negative incentives (physical punishment if the quota was not reached) and positive incentives (small monetary rewards for extra picking). In the case of cotton, this managerial strategy, combined with new cotton varieties that were easier to pick, allowed the individual harvesting capacity to increase by four between 1820 and 1860. In the case of coffee, the harvest capacity in Brazil in the 1850s was three times higher than it had been in the Caribbean in the 1780s.[22]

By the mid-nineteenth century the U.S. South showed a good level of economic development, measured in terms of transportation network, manufacturing, financial system, urbanization, and total productive capacity, a phenomenon that was much more pronounced than in the Empire of Brazil. This was due in large part to the strategic role that cotton occupied in the industrial world economy. Coffee, regardless of the social and geographic spread of its consumption, remained a stimulant that was drunk at breakfast or between meals. This asymmetry, however, did not prevent the ties between the two slave societies from deepening in the 1850s. The main market for Brazilian coffee was the United States, which paid for these imports with the resources obtained from its cotton exports to Europe. After the closing of the transatlantic slave trade to Brazil in 1850, as a result of the escalation of British naval military pressure, the United States provided a model for the continuing expansion of the slave coffee economy through internal slave trade and the natural reproduction of slaves. Above all, the power of southern slaveholders within the United States meant that their Brazilian counterparts could count on a strong ideological containment barrier for their institution in the world system. This protective wall, however, collapsed in 1861.[23]

The master class in Brazil and its political power in the Brazilian Empire were distinct from southern slaveholders' control over the antebellum U.S. federal government. The slaveholding interests that emerged with the development of the coffee complex of the Center South had been decisive for the institutional construction of the Second Reign in Brazil at the turn of the 1840s, but the emperor and the imperial political elites did not automatically follow the political platform of slave owners. In 1850, for example, under the threat of war with Britain, the Party of Order—the political mainstay of Second Slavery in the Empire of Brazil—agreed to close the transatlantic slave trade.[24]

A deeper disjunction between the imperial elite and slave planters occurred in the late 1860s. The genesis of the Free Womb Law (freeing the children of slave mothers born after 1871) reflected how the Brazilian emperor D. Pedro II and the Council of State understood the new international conjuncture that followed the end of the American Civil War and its implications in the context of the beginning of the Paraguayan War—the most serious military conflict in postcolonial South America, whose immediate cause was the dispute between the Empire of Brazil and the republics of Argentina, Uruguay, and Paraguay over the hegemony at the River Plate zone. A perception that the Empire of Brazil was profoundly isolated spread all over the diplomatic correspondence, the debates of the Council of State, the press, and the Parliament. After 1865, Brazil was the only independent country in the Western Hemisphere that still permitted black slavery. During the Paraguayan War (1864–70) the difficulties in establishing a national army as a result of the peculiarities of the Brazilian social fabric became explicit, while a new wave of republicanism unleashed in the hemisphere after the Union victory established the Empire of Brazil as a complete stranger among both its allies (Uruguay and Argentina) and its enemy (Paraguay).[25]

Fears of isolation were not necessarily unanimous among Brazilian leaders, in part because of the great prestige that the constitutional monarchy still enjoyed. But it is not a coincidence that the founding of the first Republican party in Brazil took place in 1873. And, regarding slavery, the perception of isolation deepened, stimulating, in addition to Dom Pedro II's personal initiative in directing a political solution to what was then euphemistically called the "servile question," the pioneering articulation of an abolitionist force in imperial politics. The Viscount of Rio Branco's cabinet presented a bill to the imperial parliament in 1871 that partly sought to contain this rising tide of antislavery with a gradualist measure. The reaction of the slaveholding interests was immediate. The coffee planters of Center South Brazil, who had been partially maintaining their labor force through reproduction, saw any Free Womb measure as a direct threat to their economic future. On the national level, however, the coffee planters' political power was temporarily undermined by their economic success: the internal slave trade that drew enslaved laborers to the prosperous coffee regions of Rio de Janeiro, São Paulo, and Minas Gerais in the 1850s and 1860s gradually weakened support for the institution in slave-exporting provinces. Despite the opposition of the coffee provinces, a Free Womb measure was approved in September 1871.[26]

The approval of the Free Womb Law in the specific conjuncture of the global coffee market in the early 1870s had great implications for the crisis of slavery in Brazil. Let's consider the matter first by examining the role of the United States in the global market for coffee (Table 1).

Table 1. U.S. and Brazilian coffee markets, 1871–1905 (five-year averages)

Years	Brazil in World Exports (percent)	United States in World Imports (percent)	World Production (tons)
1871–75	50.1	31.3	426.000
1876–80	47.6	34.97	512.400
1881–85	51.8	37.7	600.960
1886–90	56.8	38.1	538.320
1891–95	57.1	40.2	634.080
1896–1900	62.4	42.1	888.360
1901–5	73.8	46.8	1,032.360

Sources: Mauro Rodrigues da Cunha, "Apêndice estatístico," in *150 anos de café*, ed. Edmar Bacha and Robert Greenhill (Rio de Janeiro: Marcellino Martins and E. Johnston, 1992), tables 1.7 and 2.2; Mario Samper and Radin Fernando, "Appendix: Historical Statistics of Coffee Production and Trade from 1700 to 1960," in *The Global Coffee Economy in Africa, Asia, and Latin America, 1500–1989*, ed. William Gervase Clarence-Smith and Steven Topik (Cambridge: Cambridge University Press, 2003), 417.

A quick reading of these figures shows that the steady increase in the share of U.S. purchases of coffee in the world market was accompanied by the equally steady increase in overall production, with the exception of a brief decline in the between 1886 and 1890. Between 1871 and 1905 the expansion of the American coffee market occurred in both absolute and relative terms. The total volume of imports more than tripled, while the annual consumption per capita went from six to thirteen pounds. Three variables are important to understand these movements. In 1872 the United States reestablished its tax-free policy precisely when population growth, the spread of commercial agriculture west of the Mississippi, and the consolidation of the manufacturing belt from New England to the Midwest significantly expanded the consumer base. However, another variable accounted for the doubling of per capita consumption: new marketing strategies and the preparation of the product, with innovations such as the introduction of paper packaging for the retail sales of coffee that had already been roasted and milled, and the creation of trademarks, with several companies operating in the import and wholesale distribution on a national scale. All these changes in the coffee consumer market, which in fact sped up some trends that were already visible in the 1830s, formed a fundamental part of the profound reconfiguration of the American social and economic fabric in the aftermath of Reconstruction. "During the four decades after the Civil War," explains Michael F. Jiménez, "coffee acquired a secure niche in the consumer habits of a continentally expansive and industrializing United States."[27]

Despite the cyclical behavior that characterized the coffee market and the general decline in agricultural prices during the so-called Long Depression, coffee prices maintained their upward trend between 1873 and 1895. This was largely due to supply constraints. In the 1870s, Ceylon, the world's third-largest producer, was forced out of the market by the devastating impact of the rust disease (*Hemileia vastatrix*), which also hit the second-largest producer in the following decade, the Dutch colony of Java. At the turn of the century, Indian Ocean producers in the world market were supplanted by producers from Central and South America (Guatemala, Costa Rica, El Salvador, Honduras, Venezuela, Colombia).[28] As for the coffee colossus of the South Atlantic, rapid growth stagnated. While Brazil's annual coffee exports went from 174,000 tons between 1871 and 1875 to 322,000 tons between 1881 and 1885, in the five-year period of 1886–90 they stagnated at 221,000 tons. The critical year was 1888, when only 206,000 tons of coffee were exported—the year slavery was abolished.[29]

Some of the historical forces that brought on the crisis in Brazilian slavery were directly related to this oscillation of coffee exports. The patterns of labor and landscape management that had ensured Brazil's dominance of the world coffee market resulted in a frighteningly fast rate of depletion of environmental resources. In fact, by the mid-nineteenth century it was already possible to observe the itinerant character of Brazilian coffee growing, that is, the existence at a given moment of zones that could be classified as frontier zones (highly productive areas that were expanding), mature zones (where coffee activity had been established for some time in average levels of productivity), or decadent zones (where the huge decline in yields was evident). Since the decadent zones were the closest to export ports, they had comparative advantages in terms of transportation costs. On the other hand, the ever-shifting frontier, with increasing volumes of beans due to the higher productivity of the coffee shrubs, tended to put pressure on the transportation system—which was, until the 1860s, entirely based on mules.[30]

The problem of transportation costs plagued the Brazilian coffee economy in the 1850s, and the only viable solution was the development of the railroad network. The main obstacle remained the difficulty of climbing the sharp, steep cliffs of the Serra do Mar. Due to new techniques pioneered in Europe and the United States to surpass mountain ranges, and with the surplus of capital in the world economy for foreign investments, the railway tracks finally began, in the beginning of the 1870s, to reach both the Vale do Paraíba western zone, the oldest coffee-growing area in Brazil, and the new coffee zones of the São Paulo province. The former region had environmental problems but was well supplied with slaves, while the coffee frontiers west of São Paulo were more productive but had fewer slaves. The simultaneous arrival of the railroads in these two regions generated different effects: in the mature and decadent zones, lower transportation costs accelerated the exploitation of the existing natural resources, while in the frontier zone they raised the value of coffee lands while also increasing the demand for more enslaved laborers.

In the 1870s this problem was solved by an internal slave trade modeled on the antebellum U.S. South. In fact, the 1870s represented the peak of the internal slave trade in Brazil, with almost one hundred thousand enslaved laborers relocated to coffee plantations areas of the Center South. Still arriving in insufficient numbers to meet the demands of the world market, slaves were forced to grow more coffee shrubs, thus experiencing increasing rates of exploitation of their labor. The economic dynamism of coffee cultivation in this specific political and social conjuncture led to contradictory tendencies that ultimately undermined slavery. In response to harsh labor conditions in the new coffee frontiers, slaves expressed a rising collective resistance. Meanwhile, the emergence of the abolitionist movement also imperiled slavery. In the immediate years after the approval of the Free Womb Law, the activities of Brazilian antislavery forces significantly decreased. Slaveholders argued that the 1871 law should represent the last word of the imperial state. At the end of the decade, however, the deep frustrations with the ineffectiveness of the law to dismantle slavery, even gradually, stimulated the articulation of abolitionism on a national scale. In 1881, slaveholders acquiesced in the suspension of the interprovincial slave trade to Rio de Janeiro, São Paulo, and Minas Gerais as a temporary measure to solve the problem of slave resistance, silence abolitionists, and, above all, maintain the national commitment to the institution. The past experience of the United States, after all, had demonstrated the risks of allowing slavery to become a sectional rather than a national matter in a political environment marked by the active presence of an abolitionist movement.[31]

The prohibition of interprovincial slave trade in 1881 affected exports during the following half-decade. New coffee shrubs take five years to get into full production. The poor performance of exports from 1886 expressed the labor shortage in the new frontiers west of São Paulo, the area responsible for the expansion of the coffee belt, between 1881 and 1885. Declining production also reflected the growing strength of Brazilian abolitionism. In 1885, proslavery gradualists succeeded in enacting the Saraiva-Cotegipe Law, which only freed sexagenarians and established the principle of a future indemnity to masters. Thereafter, urban abolitionists fashioned an alliance with enslaved laborers. By late 1887 the situation in the coffee regions had become revolutionary, with mass flights organized by abolitionists, slave riots, murders of planters and overseers, and, as a response of the slave powers, the lynching of captives and abolitionists. Many planters responded to the near collapse of slavery by promising their slaves freedom in exchange for long-term labor contracts that secured the future labor force. The law of May 13, 1888, abolishing slavery immediately and without indemnity, accounted for the breakdown of the coffee harvest that year.[32]

In sum, the impasses of Brazilian slave coffee economy in the 1870s and 1880s was related to the political and economic transformations of Reconstruction in the United States in two different ways. First, the remarkable expansion of the world's largest consumer market for coffee that occurred in a context in which Asian producers abandoned the market without being immediately replaced by their Latin American counterparts kept coffee prices high. This stimulated production in Brazil, where new means of transportation opened up new frontier areas. Second, the outcome of the American Civil War profoundly transformed the social, political, and economic conditions for the survival of Brazilian slavery. The destruction of U.S. slavery and its uneven transition to emancipation and the recomposition of labor relations in the cotton plantations, shaped the perceptions of Brazilian slave planters over the nature of their own crisis.

It is important to remember that until the mid-1880s the returns obtained from investments in slaves for coffee production remained relatively unchanged. Nonetheless, the different social actors of the period (planters, slaves, freedmen, intellectuals, politicians, etc.) clearly perceived that the world built in the first half of the nineteenth century was rapidly declining. This uncertainty manifested itself in the Agricultural Congress held in Rio de Janeiro between July 8 and 10, 1878. With 456 registered planters, the Congress sought to identify possible solutions for the crisis of Brazilian slavery. They discussed alternatives: the indefinite maintenance of the institution according to the guidelines of its "natural death" provided for by the Free Womb Law; sharecropping with former slaves in case of abolition; large-scale engagement of indentured Asian laborers; and increased European immigration. They recognized that profound changes had arrived between 1865 and 1871, as a speech by a planter from the Rio de Janeiro province demonstrated:

> That the country is in a time of transition created by the law of September 28, 1871, no one will deny it. The extinction of slavery among us is a matter of time. We need to take care of this passage to another state, in the way of attracting moralized people who will come to interpose between us and the individuals who will leave

> service hungry for freedom, thus preserving us from the scenes of the United States, of its insanity and insults that may appear.[33]

It was in the sense identified by this planter—the disorder in plantations that would come from the end of the slavery if preventive measures were not taken—that the experience of the reconfiguration of labor relations in the postbellum South became a constitutive part of the experience of the crisis of slavery in Brazil.

The antebellum southern slaveholder regime dominated the world cotton market before 1861 through strict spatial control of the enslaved laborers, complete absence of autonomy to regulate personal and family time allocation, and, above all, an astonishing workload in the cotton plantations extracted through a brutal system of physical supervision and coercion. These qualities of slave labor constituted the ultimate antithesis of what enslaved people understood as freedom. "Hungry" for liberation, former slaves totally rejected the labor-management system that had been created under slavery—hence the negative expectations of all business agents regarding the immediate postwar recovery of the southern cotton economy. They concluded that if freedmen were given access to land and there was no extra-economic coercion, the South would follow the path of the British West Indies after 1838.[34] It was precisely these two problems—how to maintain the plantation system and a disciplined labor force in a postslavery world—that, in the late 1870s, shaped the thinking of Brazilian planters during the Rio de Janeiro Agricultural Congress.

Few political actors coming from the victorious side of the Civil War supported radical agrarian reform, and unfortunately this possibility was soon set aside. As for extra-economic coercion, the project to make it a rule in the postbellum South was quite concrete. The Black Codes, which most southern states enacted during Presidential Reconstruction, sought to maintain the backbone of the slave-management system in order to force former slaves to work in the cotton plantations for wages under the unified command of the planters. But the Black Codes also alarmed the Radical Republicans and found a lively response from freed rural laborers. The beginning of Radical Reconstruction, the longing of former slaves for autonomy, and the structural problem of the credit system in the postbellum South buried the project of establishing a coercive wage-labor regime. The enslaved community shared a common desire for autonomous labor, repressed under slavery, and this desire became one of the main challenges for former slaveholders aiming to restore the crux of the old labor regime. As an alternative, planters tried to keep managerial authority relatively centralized through the division of the freed labor force into separate and independent gangs, the so-called squads, regimented by foremen who acted as intermediaries between employer and employee. Their managerial problem, however, continued. In addition to having greater autonomy in the establishment of labor discipline, the squads also reduced the potential labor supply to planters by excluding women and children. Without immediate access to land ownership after the defeat of land reform, former slaves clearly preferred a tenant share system in which they had control over family time and labor. In spite of regional variations, the transition from work squads to sharecropping organized around the family became common by the early 1880s. What emerged from this conflictive process was the breakdown of the whole scheme of centralized management of the cotton labor process of slavery times.[35]

The collapse of the antebellum credit system, which was based on collaterals in enslaved human beings, combined with the ideology of family labor that motivated the former slaves, served as the other decisive variable in the establishment of sharecropping. After 1865, lacking available credit to establish a solid wage system, planters were compelled to accept the sharecropping system. However, under the changing conditions of the global cotton economy and the new social correlation of forces in the second half of the 1870s, what once was an obstacle soon became an advantage for the planter. According to the terms of the sharecropping arrangement, in times of cotton price decline the share tenant shared his losses with the planter. For recently freed black farmers, the depression after 1873 helped to transform sharecropping into a relationship in which the tenant became increasingly subjected to indebtedness. In regions such as the Mississippi Delta, the fast advance of cotton production in the 1880s was based on a pattern that was closer to wage labor, with payment in kind, than to the peasant independence of the classic tenant.[36]

The reestablishment of the regional political power of planters in the late 1870s, after the collapse of the Republican Party in the South and the end of Radical Reconstruction, enabled them to construct an increasingly coercive legal framework for black cash-and-share tenants. But the extraordinary recovery and expansion of cotton production in the postbellum United States did not come from the freedmen and their descendants.

The levels of labor exploitation prevailing at the time of slavery as measured by the area of cultivation allocated to each field worker and individual cotton-picking capacity remained a thing of the past. Cotton production during Reconstruction increasingly relied on white tenants and farmers of the upcountry, who, after the Civil War, moved from subsistence farming to commercial cotton production. White farmers thus fell prey to the same indebtedness that constrained black tenants. By 1880, white tenants and independent farmers accounted for 44 percent of the cotton supply of the South. The advance of their crops allowed total U.S. production to double during the thirty years after 1861. By that time, both small white farmers and tenants and the big landlords were subordinated, albeit asymmetrically, to the economic forces of the North. The same U.S. domestic market that absorbed increasing amounts of Brazilian coffee was now the main buyer of southern cotton as well as its main source of credit. In order to reaffirm their regional power after 1877, landlords, in a complete reversal of what had been the balance of power between the South and the Union before 1861, acquiesced in the political and economic dominance of the industrial and financial interests that had won the Civil War.[37]

As part of an uneven but combined historical process, the 1880s saw the confluence of the consolidation of sharecropping as proletarianized labor in the post-Reconstruction U.S. South and the crystallization of an alternative to free labor in the slave coffee frontier of Center South Brazil. In the critical conjuncture of the 1870s, the planters in the area west of São Paulo created a completely new form of labor organization, the *colonato*. Although distinct from southern sharecropping, both strategies tried to solve the same problem: how to recover the high levels of labor exploitation of slavery times in the post-emancipation period. Born out of a failed experiment with the sharecropping system in the São Paulo coffee frontier in the 1850s, the *colonato* solved, in a remarkable way, all the dilemmas that U.S. cotton planters faced with sharecropping. The key feature of the new system was the maintenance, with free labor, of some of the central features of the organization of the labor process and landscape management that had been created decades earlier for the employment of slave labor.

In order to describe the nature of this new arrangement we must see the images that opened this chapter. In the paintings of the Santa Gertrudes

Figure 1. Antonio Ferrigno, *Florada*, Fazenda Santa Gertrudes—Araras, SP, 1903, oil on canvas, 100 × 150 cm, Museu Paulista da USP, São Paulo.

plantation that were exhibited in Saint Louis in 1904, Antonio Ferrigno portrayed how labor had been organized in the coffee plantations of São Paulo after the abolition of slavery, representing it visually with a strong ideological perspective. The first painting of the series (Fig. 1) represented the weeding of the coffee rows with the shrubs in full bloom. Recognized in every corner of the globe as the most beautiful time of a coffee plantation, commodity production was here transmuted in aesthetic value. By observing the intensity and duration of the flowering it was possible to evaluate the volume of the coming crop. Separating the headquarters of the plantation (the white spot located at the bottom of the valley, behind the dam) from the sea of coffee shrubs planted on the hills were two long aligned rows of small white huts: these were the colonies, that is, the houses for rural laborers submitted to the *colonato* regime.

Segregated from the complex of buildings that were articulated around the quadrilateral of the *terreiros* (big house, coffee machine house, coffee barns), this new housing pattern for laborers departed from the principle of spatial organization of slave quarters (the *senzalas em quadra*) in Brazilian coffee plantations, based as they were on the prison-like confinement of slaves within that quadrilateral. This was the model of the Santa Gertrudes until the 1880s, when more than two hundred slaves lived in its slave quarters. In 1903, all its 170 families of free *colonos* (more than a thousand people) lived outside the quadrangle of the headquarters. The activity performed by the three women represented in the painting suggests that it was a non-collectivized work. In fact, under the *colonato* arrangement each settler family was responsible for a plot (*talhão*) of between two thousand and fifteen thousand coffee shrubs, depending on the number of "hoes" (*enxadas*) available in the family, that is, on the number of adults and teenagers able to work. One man was equivalent to a "hoe," with the capacity of cultivating two thousand shrubs; women and teens up to age sixteen were generally regarded as "half-hoes." Workers' main task was the weeding of the coffee rows four to six times a year. For the cultivation of the plot (*talhão*), a fixed annual salary (with biweekly or monthly installments) was paid to the head of the household, invariably a man. Ferrigno, however, chose to represent only three women weeding, suggesting that they belonged to the same family nucleus—wife, daughters, sisters.[38]

The ideological implications of the feminization of work on Ferrigno's visual representation are more explicit in the second oil (Fig. 2). In contrast to the cultivation of the *talhões*, which was organized in family units, with each of them being responsible for a fixed quantity of coffee shrubs

Figure 2. Antonio Ferrigno, *Colheita*, Fazenda Santa Gertrudes—Araras, SP, 1903, oil on canvas, 100 × 150 cm, Museu Paulista da USP, São Paulo.

for an equally fixed money payment, during harvest the members of all the *colono* families (men, women, teenagers, children) were mobilized by the managers, who would determine the number of coffee shrubs to be picked every day according to the progress of labor and the degree of maturity of the cherries on the shrubs. Thus the plots that were separately weeded by individual families would be collectively harvested by the whole workforce.

The goal here was to stimulate competition among families in order to accelerate the pace of the harvest in these enormous coffee plantations (in 1903, Santa Gertrudes contained one million coffee shrubs). In this case the payment system was per piece, that is to say, per quantity of coffee harvested individually. After the sacks of cherries were full, they were delivered to the cart driver, who gave the laborer a corresponding receipt.

After the harvest, the head of the household showed the receipts of the amount harvested by all members of his family to the managers and received his payment. Ferrigno sought to represent carefully all these elements of labor organization during harvest (the collectivized labor, entire families in the field, the sacks being filled, the wagons collecting the sacks), though he visually emphasized women. His message offered at the Saint Louis exposition was that women who belonged to stable families grew Brazilian coffee. More importantly, these were white women, a departure from the recent slave past of the Brazilian coffee economy.[39]

For the processing of coffee beans, Ferrigno chose to represent three scenes: washing the cherries that came from the field in carts, with four workers in charge of these tasks (Fig. 3); drying coffee beans in the large *terreiros* of the headquarters (on the left one sees the coffee mill barn; in the background, the big house), which male workers performed (it is possible to count thirty-six of them), supervised by a foreman (Fig. 4); and the final, fully mechanized processing (Fig. 5). Labor relations in the processing sphere were not based on the *colonato* system: all these individuals were seasonal laborers in the *plantation*, hired for fixed wages only for the harvest period. Women and children were not employed. Ferrigno's focus here was on the technification of the production process—the goal in Saint Louis, after all, was to propagandize the quality of Brazilian coffee. In order to account for the enormous volume of beans collected by the *derriça* system—that is, the indiscriminate harvesting of both green and ripe coffee cherries—Santa Gertrudes combined the wet system (immediate pulping of the cherries that came from the fields, drying them

Figure 3. Antonio Ferrigno, *Lavadouro*, Fazenda Santa Gertrudes—Araras, SP, 1903, oil on canvas, 100 × 150 cm, Museu Paulista da USP, São Paulo.

Figure 4. Antonio Ferrigno, *O terreiro*, Fazenda Santa Gertrudes—Araras, SP, 1903, oil on canvas, 100 × 150 cm, Museu Paulista da USP, São Paulo.

Figure 5. Antonio Ferrigno, *Ensacamento do café*, Fazenda Santa Gertrudes—Araras, SP, 1903, oil on canvas, 100 × 150 cm, Museu Paulista da USP, São Paulo.

afterward) and the dry system (drying of the cherries in the drying fields with the pulp on). This combination of techniques was an innovation of the Brazilian slave coffee economy, which was greatly improved in the last three decades of the nineteenth century (i.e., before and after the law of May 13, 1888). It allowed large plantations to produce coffee of different qualities—and, consequently, of different prices—within the same unit, maximizing the labor productivity in the field by allocating as many coffee shrubs as possible per field worker and accelerating the pace of the harvest via monetary incentives.[40]

Unlike the transition to sharecropping in the U.S. South, the *colonato* maintained the slave organization of the labor process in several crucial aspects. Centralization of managerial decisions over labor and production processes, collective labor under a unified command at critical moments of these processes, extraction of a great workload in weeding and harvesting, technification of the processing of beans articulated to the maximization of labor time in the fields became common characteristics of the Brazilian coffee plantation under slavery and under the *colonato*. It is true that under the *colonato* the field worker cultivated far fewer coffee shrubs than a slave (two thousand versus four thousand shrubs). But if the constant supply of free labor was guaranteed, the problem of individual decrease in output per worker would be more than compensated for by the end of the rigidity of fixed capital that always accompanied the purchase of a slave. Moreover, the problem of overseeing labor under the *colonato* was solved to a large extent by the internalization of supervision by the families themselves: the heads of families had to establish how much their relatives would be able to cultivate and harvest. Finally, there was the practice of non-monetary payment, that is, the permission for families to grow food (basically corn and beans) between the rows of the new coffee plantations or in remote lands. The product of these food plots belonged entirely to the *colonos*, and this was the basis of their subsistence. This mechanism allowed planters to decrease the amount of wages paid for the cultivation of the *talhões*.[41]

The labor system just described through the paintings that Antonio Ferrigno composed in 1903 was already established in the early 1880s, at the peak of the crisis of Brazilian slavery, which took place in a moment of the world economy favorable to coffee. The *colonato* had been created and used on a small scale in large plantations west of São Paulo that still employed slaves as the basis of their labor force. In other words, the planters of the coffee frontiers of São Paulo already had a system of work alternative to slavery, but they lacked workers. Considering the historical experience of former slaves who refused to work permanently with their wives and children in the same units where they had been enslaved if there were minimal alternatives for survival outside these plantations (as was the case west of São Paulo in the late nineteenth century, with an open frontier), and especially considering the fact that the new coffee plantations were being founded in zones of low population density, the solution to the problem of the supply of laborers to the *colonato* system could only be found in the international labor market. The experience after 1888 would confirm the inelasticity of the engagement of black workers to the *colonato*. However, as seasonal wage laborers, the former slaves and their descendants were mobilized more frequently, as Ferrigno recorded in his painting on the departure of coffee to the train station (Fig. 6).[42]

Brazilian coffee planters knew that without some kind of public or private subsidy, European or Asian immigrants would not come to Brazil. The basis for this conclusion lay not only in the Brazilian experience but also in the observation of the American experience: before the Civil War, immigrants avoided the South because of the presence of slavery, choosing instead the North. Slave zones—like Brazil in the 1870s and

Figure 6. Antonio Ferrigno, *Café para a estação*, Fazenda Santa Gertrudes—Araras, SP, 1903, oil on canvas, 100 × 150 cm, Museu Paulista da USP, São Paulo.

1880s—discouraged voluntary immigration. Even after the end of slavery, however, the U.S. South failed to connect itself to the international labor market once it became crystallized as a region of low wages in a country marked by high wages.[43]

In short, for the *colonato* to work there was a need to find in the global labor market a new source of laborers that could be attracted to Brazil. At the crucial moment of the abolitionist revolution of 1887–88, the solution had already been found. Among the absences of the 1878 Agricultural Congress in Rio de Janeiro, perhaps the most notable were those of the brothers Antônio and Martinho Prado Jr., planters of the coffee frontier west of São Paulo and important figures (although members of different party associations) in provincial and imperial politics. That same year, the group of planters led by them sent emissaries to Europe to investigate which countries could provide emigrants for the province. Northern Italy—more specifically the Veneto region—served as the region with the greatest potential to provide the necessary workforce for the *colonato* system.[44]

The profound impact of the rise of post-Reconstruction agriculture in the U.S. Midwest on the world grain market generated human surpluses in Italy that the São Paulo coffee planters could exploit through a subsidized immigration project. The foundations of midwestern agriculture's growth during the Long Reconstruction were established before the Civil War, contributing to growing sectional polarization. We only need to remember how the expansion of antebellum Chicago's grain, lumber, and meat industries provided one of the main electoral bases of the Republican Party and therefore of the election of Abraham Lincoln. The victory of the Union accelerated the consolidation of the U.S. domestic market, and the Homestead Act (1862) offered vast new areas for East Coast and European farmers attracted by the free land in the prairie region. The prosperity of agrarian capitalism in the Midwest during the Reconstruction era had two important implications. On the one hand, the Midwest helped to expand the consumer market for Brazilian coffee. On the other hand, its oversupply of grain was the key force that caused a threefold decrease in world wheat prices between 1867 and 1894, completely rearranging the global market. The reorganization of midwestern family farms, a result of mechanization of the production process, allowed U.S. producers to cope successfully with the depression in grain prices, but in Europe its effects were devastating. The grain invasion from the United States, as well as from Ukraine, Australia, and Argentina, fell hard on family farming in Europe. In the case of Italy, the situation grew even worse because of the tariff changes that were introduced by Unification, breaking the security of independent peasant, tenant, and proletarian families. In the crucial decades of the 1870s and 1880s, one of the most affected regions was the Veneto.[45]

Thus the laborers needed for the *colonato* system were made available by the global consequences of the Civil War and Reconstruction, the crucial events of the systemic crisis of the Second Slavery. Coffee planters in the São Paulo frontiers were particularly well prepared for it, unlike planters in the declining areas of the Paraíba Valley. The itinerant character of the Brazilian coffee economy had produced a split in the old master class. Already perceptible in the late 1870s, it became more explicit at a moment of truth that occurred during the 1887–88 revolution. Clear signs of the loss of competitiveness of the former producing zones of the Vale do Paraíba, such as environmental depletion and growing indebtedness with banks and commissioners, led its planters to cling to the platform of compensation in the event of abolition—another ghost of the American Civil War that frightened them. Planters of the São Paulo western frontier, with large reserves of virgin land and an open credit portfolio, rejected compensation for what it would entail in fiscal terms. The abolition of slavery without compensation destroyed the remaining political capital of the constitutional monarchy among one of its harshest bastions, the planters of the Paraíba Valley, paving the way for the military coup that a year later installed a Republican regime in Brazil. The Republican Paulista Party, founded in 1873 and largely based on the coffee-growing zones of the frontier, assumed control of the federal government: the first three civilian presidents of Brazil, who ruled from 1894 to 1906, were all coffee planters belonging to party cadres.[46]

The federalist arrangement established by the Republican Constitution of 1891, inspired by the American model of 1787, granted broad autonomy for the states to regulate fiscal and budgetary matters, a historical demand of coffee planters from São Paulo in view of the needs of credit organization and, above all, for the continuity of the subsidized immigration that had been started in the final years of the empire. In 1886 they had founded the Sociedade Promotora de Imigração (SPI; Society for Immigration Promotion), a nonprofit private entity hired by the provincial government to recruit families for the *colonato* system, offering them fully subsidized tickets from their villages in rural Italy to the gates of coffee plantations in São Paulo. With the proclamation of the republic, this policy became official with the establishment of a state tax on coffee exports that created a fund to pay transatlantic travel expenses to the *colonato* families. As slavery and the monarchy were definitively buried, the SPI was dissolved and its attributions were fully incorporated by the State of São Paulo.[47]

The influx of Italians who entered São Paulo between 1886 and 1903 through this system of subsidized labor provided the basis for the astonishing leap in Brazil's coffee exports, thus overcoming the growth slumps of the first half of the 1880s. Between 1886 and 1896, São Paulo became the largest receiver of Italian immigrants in the Americas, surpassing the United States and Argentina. In order to feed the *colonato* machine, 80 percent of them arrived at the port of Santos through the scheme of full subsidy of travel expenses. The Italian families who entered this new labor regime were the ones that visitors could observe in the Brazilian Pavilion at the Louisiana Purchase Exposition—between 1895 and 1930, 65 percent of Santa Gertrudes *colonos* had been born in Italy, against 20 percent of Portuguese and 10 percent of Spaniards. State control over the reproduction of the labor force of the *colonato* system ensured that the wages paid to the coffee workers remained stable until the outbreak of World War I. It was this cheap labor supply that encouraged São Paulo planters to expand coffee frontiers constantly, generating the problem of overproduction and falling prices that their representatives were trying to solve through coffee advertising in Saint Louis in 1904.[48]

State intervention in the formation of the labor force for the *colonato* system acquired the clear character of a subsidy for the coffee capital. The contrast with the U.S. South is truly remarkable, as Steven Hahn showed in his pioneering 1990 articles. The power that São Paulo planters maintained and consolidated with the end of slavery and the construction of the Republican regime allowed them to re-create the extraterritoriality of the labor market for the plantation economy, in a clear reinvention—under the new historical circumstances of global capitalism—of the structural role that the transatlantic slave trade had played until 1850. What was lacking in Hahn's original argument, and what this chapter has attempted to show, is how this result was shaped by the abolition of slavery in the United States, or in other words, how the reconfiguration of the North American capitalist order in the Reconstruction era was an essential constituent part of the crisis of the Second Slavery and the passage from empire to republic in Brazil.

Acknowledgments

I would like to thank Leonardo Marques, Alain El Youssef, Waldomiro Lourenço da Silva Jr., Tâmis Parron, Dale Tomich, Jeffrey D. Needell, and William A. Link for their various comments. This chapter is partially the result of a larger research project founded by CNPq, the Brazilian research council, of which I am a fellow.

Notes

1. On the history of the Brazilian participation in Saint Louis and the construction of its pavilion, see Oirgres Leici Cordeiro de Macedo, "Construção diplomática, missão arquitetônica: Os Pavilhões do Brasil nas Feiras Internacionais de Saint Louis (1904) e Nova York (1939)" (PhD diss., Faculdade de Arquitetura e Urbanismo da Universidade de São Paulo, 2012), 14–54.

2. "Giant new rituals of self-congratulation" is how Eric Hobsbawm (*The Age of Capital, 1848–1875* [London: Weidenfeld & Nicolson, 1975], 47) defines the practice of the nineteenth-century universal exhibition. See also Jürgen Osterhammel, *The Transformation of the World: A Global History of the Nineteenth Century* (Princeton: Princeton University Press, 2014), 14–15; Margarida de Souza Neves, *As vitrines do progresso* (Rio

de Janeiro: PUC, 1986); and Sandra J. Pesavento, *Exposições universais: Espetáculo da modernidade do século XIX* (São Paulo: Hucitec, 1997).

3. Robert W. Rydell, *All the World's a Fair: Visions of Empire at American International Expositions, 1876–1916* (Chicago: University of Chicago Press, 1984), 256–303.

4. On the role of the *paulista* coffee interests during the First Republic, see Joseph L. Love, *São Paulo in the Brazilian Federation, 1889–1937* (Stanford: Stanford University Press, 1980). On the general context of the coffee valorization policy, see Thomas H. Holloway, *Vida e morte do Convênio de Taubaté: A primeira valorização do café* (Rio de Janeiro: Paz & Terra, 1978). On coffee prices, see Comissão à Exposição Universal da Compra da Louisiana 1904, *Relatório Apresentado ao exmo. Sr. Dr. Lauro Severiano* Müller, *Ministro da Indústria, Viação e Obras Públicas, pelo gal. F. M. de Souza Aguiar, Presidente da Comissão* (Rio de Janeiro: Imprensa Nacional, 1905), 388–90; Mauro Rodrigues da Cunha, "Apêndice estatístico," in *150 anos de café*, ed. Edmar Bacha and Robert Greenhill (Rio de Janeiro: Marcellino Martins and E. Johnston, 1992), 283–391; Steven Topik, "The Integration of the World Coffee Market," in *The Global Coffee Economy in Africa, Asia, and Latin America, 1500–1989,* ed. William Gervase Clarence-Smith and Steven Topik (Cambridge: Cambridge University Press, 2003), 21–49; and Mark Pendergrast, *Uncommon Grounds: The History of Coffee and How It Transformed the World*, rev. ed. (New York: Basic Books, 2010), 21–72.

5. "Exposição de S. Luiz," *Correio Paulistano,* November 19, 1903, 3.

6. On the Santa Gertrudes plantation, see Maria Silvia C. Beozzo Bassanezi, "Fazenda Santa Gertrudes: Uma abordagem quantitativa das relações de trabalho, em uma propriedade rural paulista, 1895–1930" (PhD diss., Faculdade de Filosofia, Ciência e Letras, Rio Claro, 1973); and Alexandre Luiz Rocha, "Fazenda Santa Gertrudes: Modelo de produção cafeeira no Oeste Paulista, 1885–1930" (PhD diss., Faculdade de Arquitetura e Urbanismo da Universidade de São Paulo, 2008). On the artist, see the catalog *Antonio Ferrigno, 100 anos depois* (São Paulo: Pinacoteca do Estado de São Paulo, 2005). On the photographs at the Agriculture Pavilion, see Francisco Marcellino de Souza Aguiar, *Brazil at the Louisiana Purchase Exposition, St. Louis, 1904* (Saint Louis: Art Dept. Saml. F. Myerson Ptg. Co., 1904), 32, 119. On the local press see the article of the *Saint Louis Republic,* October 9, 1904, translated and published in Comissão à Exposição Universal da Compra da Louisiana 1904, *Relatório,* 388–90.

7. W.E.B. Du Bois, *Black Reconstruction in America, 1860–1880* (1935; New York: Atheneum, 1992), 15. Bruce E. Baker and Brian Kelly highlight Du Bois's innovation in their introduction to their edited volume *After Slavery: Race, Labor, and Citizenship in the Reconstruction South* (Gainesville: University Press of Florida, 2013), 4.

8. Among the exceptions are C. Vann Woodward's "The Price of Freedom" in *What Was Freedom's Price?* ed. David S. Sansing (Jackson: University of Mississippi Press, 1978), 93–113. Eric Foner's framework in *Nothing but Freedom: Emancipation and Its Legacy* (Baton Rouge: Louisiana State University Press, 1983) found a long development in Edward Bartlett Rugemer's *The Problem of Emancipation: The Caribbean Roots of the American Civil War* (Baton Rouge: Louisiana State University Press, 2008).

9. Steven Hahn, "Emancipation and the Development of Capitalist Agriculture:

The South in Comparative Perspective," in *What Made the South Different?* ed. Kees Gispen (Jackson: University Press of Mississippi, 1990), 71–88; Steven Hahn, "Class and State in Postemancipation Societies: Southern Planters in Comparative Perspective," *American Historical Review* 95, no. 1 (February 1990): 75–98

.

10. Hahn, "Class and State," 88, 98.

11. It is important to note that Jeffrey R. Kerr-Ritchie ("Was U.S. Emancipation Exceptional in the Atlantic, or Other Worlds?" in *The American South and the Atlantic World,* ed. Brian Ward, Martyn Bone, and William A. Link [Gainesville: University Press of Florida, 2013], 149–69) concludes his article by pointing out that "comparative US emancipation studies ignore connections between the United States and emancipation elsewhere in the Americas" (164). In spite of this observation, in this article he offered few materials to account for such a demand.

12. Such are the cases of David T. Gleeson and Simon Lewis, eds., *The Civil War as Global Conflict* (Columbia: University of South Carolina Press, 2014); Jörg Nagler, Don H. Doyle, and Marcus Gräser, eds., *The Transnational Significance of the American Civil War* (London: Palgrave MacMillan, 2016); and Don H. Doyle, ed., *American Civil Wars: The United States, Latin America, Europe, and the Crisis of the 1860s* (Chapel Hill: University of North Carolina Press, 2017). In the specific field of global history, see also Sven Beckert, *Empire of Cotton: A Global History* (New York: Knopf, 2014). In diplomatic relations, see Don H. Doyle, *The Cause of All Nations: An International History of the American Civil War* (New York: Basic Books, 2015); and Matthew Karp, *This Vast Southern Empire: Slaveholders and the Helm of American Foreign Policy* (Cambridge: Harvard University Press, 2016). For a good synthesis of this program to enlarge the spatial scope of the history of slavery and postslavery toward a more sustained comparative history, see also Enrico Dal Lago, *American Slavery, Atlantic Slavery, and Beyond: The U.S. "Peculiar Institution" in International Perspective* (Boulder: Paradigm, 2012).

13. David Blight (*Race and Reunion: The Civil War in American Memory* [Cambridge: Belknap Press, 2001]) and Steven Hahn (*A Nation under Our Feet: Black Political Struggles in the Rural South from Slavery to the Great Migration* [Cambridge: Belknap Press, 2003]) were among the first to defend this temporal enlargement of the Reconstruction. The agenda was soon incorporated by the chapter published in the volume edited by Thomas J. Brown, *Reconstructions: New Perspectives on the Postbellum United States* (New York: Oxford University Press, 2006). As Foner warns us, "the implication of this chronological redefinition is significant. Historians now recognize Reconstruction as part of the long trajectory *of Southern* and national history, not a bizarre aberration unrelated to what came before or after, as the Dunning School saw it. We now have what might be called a Long Reconstruction, like the long civil rights movement (which begins in the 1930s and 1940s) or the long nineteenth century (1789–1914)." Foner, Afterword, in Baker and Kelly, *After Slavery,* 224. The same point is restated by William A. Link and James Broomall in their introduction to their edited volume *Rethinking American Emancipation: Legacies of Slavery and the Quest for Black Freedom* (Cambridge: Cambridge University Press, 2016)

and by the recent synthesis of Steven Hahn, *A Nation without Borders: The United States and Its World in an Age of Civil Wars, 1830–1910* (New York: Viking, 2016).

14. Steven Hahn, "What Sort of World Did the Civil War Make?" in *The World the Civil War Made*, ed. Gregory P. Downs and Kate Masur (Chapel Hill: University of North Carolina Press, 2015), 247.

15. The literature that applies the concept is already vast. For a recent evaluation that has essays by Robin Blackburn, Dale Tomich, Rafael Marquese, Ricardo Salles, José Antonio Piqueras, and Edward E. Baptist, see the volume edited by Rafael Marquese and Ricardo Salles, *Escravidão e capitalismo histórico no século XIX: Cuba, Brasil e Estados Unidos* (Rio de Janeiro: Civilização Brasileira, 2016).

16. Dale W. Tomich, *Through the Prism of Slavery: Labor, Capital, and World Economy* (Boulder: Rowman & Littlefield, 2004), 61.

17. According to the Braudelian notion of time that informs the proposal of the Second Slavery, structures and events are conceived in a dialectical way. In Reinhart Koselleck's formulation sharing the Braudelian program, "more or less enduring, or longer-term structures, are the conditions of possible events. . . . Conversely, structures are comprehensible only in the medium of the events within which structures are articulated, and which are tangible as structures within them." Koselleck, *Futures Past: On the Semantics of Historical Time* (New York: Columbia University Press, 2004), 109. On the potentialities of the Second Slavery perspective for the practice of global history, see the notes of Sebastian Conrad, *What Is Global History?* (Princeton: Princeton University Press, 2016), 52.

18. Rafael Marquese and Tâmis Parron, "International Proslavery: The Politics of the Second Slavery," in *The Politics of the Second Slavery*, ed. Dale Tomich (Binghamton: SUNY Press, 2016), 25–56.

19. On the free-trade platform of cotton exporters, see Brian Schoen, *The Fragile Fabric of the Union: Cotton, Federal Politics, and the Global Origins of the Civil War* (Baltimore: Johns Hopkins University Press, 2009), chap. 3. On coffee, see Tâmis Parron, "A política da escravidão na era da liberdade: Estados Unidos, Brasil e Cuba, 1787–1846" (PhD diss., Programa de História Social da Universidade de São Paulo, 2015), chap. 5; and Steven Topik and Michelle Craig McDonald, "Why Americans Drink Coffee: The Boston Tea Party or Brazilian Slavery?" in *Coffee: A Comprehensive Guide to the Bean, the Beverage, and the Industry*, ed. Robert W. Thurston, Jonathan Morris, and Shawn Steinman (Boulder: Rowman & Littlefield, 2013), 234–47.

20. Afonso d'Escragnolle Taunay, *História do café no Brasil* (Rio de Janeiro: DNC, 1939), 4:121–22; Cunha, "Apêndice estatístico," 330.

21. On the volume of cotton production, see Stuart Bruchey, *Cotton and the Growth of the American Economy, 1790–1860: Sources and Readings* (New York: Harcourt, Brace & World, 1967); on coffee, see Cunha, "Apêndice estatístico." On the spatial and human mobility of the cotton and coffee slave economies, see Edward E. Baptist, *The Half Has Never Been Told: Slavery and the Making of American Capitalism* (New York: Basic Books, 2014); and Rafael Marquese, "Capitalism, Slavery, and the Brazilian Coffee Economy," in *The Legacy of Eric Williams, Caribbean Scholar and Statesman*, ed. Colin Palmer (Mona: University of the West Indies Press, 2015), 190–223.

22. John Hebron Moore, *Agriculture in Antebellum Mississippi* (1958; New York: Octagon Books, 1971), 112; Reinhold Teuscher, *Algumas observações sobre a estadistica sanitária dos escravos em fazendas de café* (Rio de Janeiro: Const. de J. Villeneuve e Comp., 1853), 4; Walter Johnson, *River of Dark Dreams: Slavery and Empire in the Cotton Kingdom* (Cambridge: Belknap Press, 2013), 151–75; Alan L. Olmstead and Paul W. Rhodes, *Creating Abundance: Biological Innovation and American Agricultural Development* (Cambridge: Cambridge University Press, 2008), 98–133; Edward E. Baptist, "Toward a Political Economy of Slave Labor: Whipping-Machines, and Modern Power," in *Slavery's Capitalism: A New History of American Economic Development*, ed. Sven Beckert and Seth Rockman (Philadelphia: University of Pennsylvania Press, 2016), 31–61; Baptist, *The Half Has Never Been Told*, 111–14; Rafael de Bivar Marquese, "African Diaspora, Slavery, and the Paraiba Valley Coffee Plantation Landscape: Nineteenth-Century Brasil," *Review (Fernand Braudel Center)* 31, no. 2 (2008): 195–216; Rafael de Bivar Marquese, "O Vale do Paraíba cafeeiro e o regime visual da Segunda Escravidão: Caso da fazenda Resgate," *Anais do Museu Paulista* 18, no. 1 (2010): 83–128.

23. For an illuminating comparison of the performance of the two economies, see Richard Graham, "Economics or Culture? The Development of US South and Brazil in the Days of Slavery," in Gispen, *What Made the South Different?* 97–124. For the internal slave trade and slave management, see Robert W. Slenes, "The Brazilian Internal Slave Trade, 1850–1888: Regional Economies, Slave Experience, and the Politics of a Peculiar Market," in *The Chattel Principle: Internal Slave Trades in the Americas*, ed. Walter Johnson (New Haven: Yale University Press, 2004), 324–70; Rafael de Bivar Marquese, *Feitores do corpo, missionários da mente: Senhores, letrados e o controle dos escravos nas Américas, 1660–1860* (São Paulo: Companhia das Letras, 2004), 259–98; Ricardo Salles, *E o Vale era o Escravo: Vassouras, século XIX: Senhores e escravos no coração do Império* (Rio de Janeiro: Civilização Brasileira, 2008), 237–71; and Marquese and Parron, "International Proslavery."

24. For the relations between the political structure of the Second Reign and the Brazilian slave society, see Jeffrey D. Needell, *The Party of Order: The Conservatives, the State, and Slavery in the Brazilian Monarchy, 1831–1871* (Stanford: Stanford University Press, 2006); Ricardo Salles, "O Império do Brasil no contexto do século XIX: Escravidão nacional, classe senhorial e intelectuais na formação do Estado," *Almanack*, no. 4 (2012): 5–45; Alain El Youssef, Bruno Fabris Stefanes, and Tâmis Parron, "Vale Expandido: Contrabando negreiro, consenso e regime representativo no Império do Brasil," in *O Vale do Paraíba e o Império do Brasil nos Quadros da Segunda Escravidão*, ed. Mariana Muaze and Ricardo Salles (Rio de Janeiro: 7 Letras, 2015), 130–56. On the differences between the politics of slavery in Brazil and the United States, see Parron, "A política da escravidão na era da liberdade," 349–451.

25. On the impact of the Civil War, see Rafael Marquese, "The Civil War in the United States and the Crisis of Slavery in Brazil," in Doyle, *American Civil Wars*, 222–45. For the impacts of the Paraguayan War on slavery in Brazil see Ricardo Salles, *Guerra do Paraguai: Escravidão e cidadania na formação do Exército* (Rio de Janeiro: Paz & Terra, 1990); and Wilma Peres Costa, *A espada de Dâmocles: O Exército, a Guerra do Paraguai e a crise do império* (São Paulo: Hucitec, 1996). For a study that compares the drafting

of former slaves by the Brazilian and American armies during the Paraguayan War and the American Civil War, see Vitor Izecksohn, *Slavery and War in the Americas: Race, Citizenship, and State Building in the United States and Brasil, 1861–1870* (Charlottesville: University Press of Virginia, 2014).

26. Marquese, "The Civil War," 233–35; Needell, *The Party of Order*, 272–314; Salles, *E o Vale era o Escravo*, 237–71; Robert Conrad, *The Destruction of Brazilian Slavery, 1850–1888* (Berkeley: University of California Press, 1972), 112–31; Ângela Alonso, *Flores, balas e votos: O movimento abolicionista brasileiro (1868–1888)* (São Paulo: Companhia das Letras, 2015); Bruno da Fonseca Miranda, "O Vale do Paraíba Cafeeiro contra a Lei do Ventre Livre, 1865–1871" (master's thesis, Universidade de São Paulo, 2018).

27. Michael F. Jiménez, "'From Plantation to Cup': Coffee and Capitalism in the United States, 1830–1930," in *Coffee, Society and Power in Latin America*, ed. William Roseberry, Lowell Gudmundson, and Mario Samper Kutschbach (Baltimore: Johns Hopkins University Press, 1995), 40; Hahn, *A Nation without Borders*, 317–61.

28. On the coffee cyclical prices, see Antônio Delfim Netto, *O problema do café no Brasil* (São Paulo: Unesp-Facamp, 2009), 20–21; and Edmar Bacha, "Política Brasileira do café: Uma avaliação centenária," in Bacha and Greenhill, *150 anos de café*, 20. For a general overview of the global coffee markets, see Clarence-Smith and Topik, *Global Coffee Economy.*

29. Mario Samper and Radin Fernando, "Appendix: Historical Statistics of Coffee Production and Trade from 100 to 1960," in Clarence-Smith and Topik, *Global Coffee Economy*, 433.

30. On the moving character of the Brazilian coffee economy, see Antonio Barros de Castro, *Sete ensaios sobre a economia brasileira* (Rio de Janeiro: Forense, 1971), 2:60–61. On the relationship between the new commodity frontiers and transportation systems, see Paul S. Ciccantell and Stephen G. Bunker, "Introduction: Space, Transport, and World-Systems Theory," in *Space and Transport in the World-System*, ed. Paul S. Ciccantell and Stephen G. Bunker (Westport, CN: Greenwood Press, 1998), 7–11. For the other topics in this and the next two paragraphs, see Marquese, "Capitalism, Slavery, and the Brazilian Coffee Economy," 196–205.

31. On the internal slave trade volume during the 1870s, see Slenes, "The Brazilian Internal Slave Trade," 338–40. For the slave resistance, see Maria Helena P. T. Machado, *Crime e escravidão: Trabalho, luta e resistência nas lavouras paulistas, 1830–1888* (São Paulo: Brasiliense, 1987), and Hebe Maria Mattos de Castro, *Das cores do silêncio: Os significados da liberdade no Sudeste escravista–Brasil, século XIX* (Rio de Janeiro: Arquivo Nacional, 1995), 137–38. On the 1881 laws, see Célia Maria Marinho Azevedo, *Onda negra, medo branco: O negro no imaginário das elites, século XIX* (Rio de Janeiro: Paz & Terra, 1987), 114–58.

32. For the new abolitionist movement, see Alonso, *Flores, votos e balas*, 304–29. For a more encompassing treatment of the alliance of abolitionists and slaves during the 1887–88 revolution, see Robert Brent Toplin, *The Abolition of Slavery in Brasil* (New York: Atheneum, 1975), 178–246.

33. João Baptista Braziel, "1a Sessão em 8 de Julho de 1878," in *Congresso Agrícola: Edição fac-similar dos anais do Congresso Agrícola, realizado no Rio de Janeiro, em 1878*, ed.

José Murilo de Carvalho (Rio de Janeiro: Fundação Casa de Rui Barbosa, 1988), 142. On the slave coffee economy rentability during the 1880s, see Pedro Carvalho de Mello and Robert W. Slenes, "Análise econômica da escravidão no Brasil," in *Economia brasileira: Uma visão histórica,* ed. Paulo Neuhaus (Rio de Janeiro: Campus, 1980), 89–122.

34. Gerald David Jaynes, *Branches without Roots: Genesis of the Black Working Class in the American South, 1862–1882* (Oxford: Oxford University Press, 1986), 9–15; Eric Foner, *Reconstruction: America's Unfinished Revolution, 1863–1877* (New York: Harper & Row, 1988), 124–75; Foner, *Nothing but Freedom*; Beckert, *Empire of Cotton,* 274–76.

35. Jaynes, *Branches without Roots,* 93–190; Gavin Wright, *Old South, New South: Revolutions in the Southern Economy since the Civil War* (Baton Rouge: Louisiana State University Press, 1986), 84–90.

36. Jaynes, *Branches without Roots,* 31, 49, 218; Foner, *Reconstruction,* 409; James C. Cobb, *The Most Southern Place on Earth: The Mississippi Delta and the Roots of Regional Identity* (Oxford: Oxford University Press, 1992), 82–101.

37. Beckert, *Empire of Cotton,* 289–92; Wright, *Old South, New South,* 34–35, 107; Foner, *Reconstruction,* 392–409; Harold Woodman, "The Political Economy of the New South: Retrospects and Prospects," *Journal of Southern History* 67, no. 4 (2001): 789–810.

38. On the spatial reconfiguration of workers' housing, see Wladimir Benicasa, "Fazenda paulista: Arquitetura rural no ciclo cafeeiro" (Tese de doutorado em arquitetura, Escola de Engenharia de São Carlos, Universidade de São Paulo, 2007), 277–312; see also Bassanezi, "A Fazenda Santa Gerrudes," 182; C. F. Van Delden Laërne, *Brazil and Java: Report on Coffee-Culture in America, Asia, and Africa* (London: W. H. Allen, 1885), 334–35; Thomas H. Holloway, *Imigrantes para o café: Café e sociedade em* São Paulo, 1886–*1934* (Rio de Janeiro: Paz & Terra, 1984), 117–18; and Verena Stolcke and Michael Hall, "A introdução do trabalho livre nas fazendas de café de São Paulo," *Revista Brasileira de História* 6 (September 1983): 80–120.

39. Bassanezi, "A fazenda Santa Gertrudes"; Holloway, *Imigrantes para o café,* 118–19.

40. On the conjugation of wet and dry systems, see Renata Cipolli D'Arbo, "Desenvolvimento tecnológico na agricultura cafeeira em São Paulo e Ribeirão Preto, 1875–1910" (PhD diss., História Econômica, Universidade de São Paulo, 2014). On seasonal labor, Cláudia Alessandra Tessari, *Braços para a colheita: Sazonalidade e permanência do trabalho temporário na agricultura paulista (1890–1915)* (São Paulo: Alameda, 2012), 210.

41. José de Souza Martins, *O cativeiro da terra* (São Paulo: Contexto, 2010), 73–76.

42. On the employment of former slaves in the coffee economy of the *paulista* frontier, and its harsh racial relations with the Italian migrants, see Karl Monsma, *A reprodução do racismo: Fazendeiros, negros e imigrantes no oeste paulista, 1880–1914* (São Carlos: EdUFSCar, 2016).

43. For the genesis of the *colonato* system within the slave coffee plantations west of São Paulo, see Stolcke and Hall, "A introdução do trabalho livre," 99–105; on the southern labor market, see Wright, *Old South, New South,* 74–76.

44. Darrell Levi, *The Prados of São Paulo, Brazil: An Elite Family and Social Change, 1840–1930* (Athens: University of Georgia Press, 1987); Zuleika M. F. Alvim, *Brava Gente! Os italianos em São Paulo, 1870–1920* (São Paulo: Brasiliense, 1986), 47; Holloway, *Imigrantes para o café,* 64–116.

45. For a more detailed exposition of this argument, see Marquese, "Capitalism, Slavery, and the Brazilian Coffee Economy," 205–10. On the Midwest takeoff and the U.S. politics, D. W. Meinig, *The Shaping of America: A Geographical Perspective on 500 Years of History,* vol. 2, *Continental America, 1800–1867* (New Haven: Yale University Press, 1993), 323–34; William Cronon, *Nature's Metropolis: Chicago and the Great West* (New York: Norton, 1991), 65–70; and John Ashworth, *Slavery, Capitalism and Politics in the Antebellum Republic,* vol. 2, *The Coming of the Civil War, 1850–1861* (Cambridge: Cambridge University Press, 2008). On the reconfiguration of the world market and the U.S. internal market after 1865, see Giovanni Arrighi, *O longo século XX: Dinheiro, poder e as origens de nosso tempo* (Rio de Janeiro: Contraponto, 1996), 300–320; Harriet Friedmann, "World Market, State, and Family Farm: Social Bases of Household Production in the Era of Wage Labor," *Comparative Studies in Society and History* 20, no. 4 (1978): 545–86; M. E. Falkus, "Russia and the International Wheat Trade, 1861–1914," *Economica,* n.s., 33, no. 132 (1966): 416–29; Morton Rothstein, "America in the International Rivalry for the British Wheat Market, 1860–1914," *Mississippi Valley Historical Review* 47, no. 3 (1960): 401–18; and Kevin H. O'Rourke, "The European Grain Invasion, 1870–1913," *Journal of Economic History* 57, no. 4 (1997): 775–801. On Italian migration, see Emilio Franzina, *A grande emigração: O êxodo dos italianos do Vêneto para o Brasil* (Campinas: Editora da UNICAMP, 2006).

46. Toplin, *Abolition of Slavery in Brasil,* 233–52; Joseph Love, "Autonomia e interdependência: São Paulo e a Federação Brasileira, 1889–1937," in *História geral da civilização brasileira,* tomo III, *O Brasil Republicano,* volume I, *Estrutura de poder e economia (1889–1930),* ed. Boris Fausto (São Paulo: Bertrand Brasil, 1989), 53–76; José E. Casalecchi, *O Partido Republicano Paulista: Política e poder (1889–1926)* (São Paulo: Brasiliense, 1987).

47. Holloway, *Imigrantes para o café,* 61–67; Martins, *O cativeiro da terra,* 59.

48. Riccardo Faini and Alessandra Venturini, "Italian Emigration in the Pre-war Period," in *Migration and the International Labor Market, 1850–1939,* ed. Jeffrey G. Williamson and Timothy J. Hatton (London: Routledge, 1994), 76; Holloway, *Imigrantes para o café,* 76–77; Martins, *O cativeiro da terra,* 59–82; Tessari, *Braços para a colheita,* 214–20; Bassanezi, "Fazenda Santa Gertrudes," 141.

2

Reconstruction and Anti-imperialism

The United States and Mexico

DON H. DOYLE

The story of the United States' postwar Reconstruction era is usually told within a tightly bound national narrative wholly disconnected from the world beyond.[1] Even as recent scholarship seeks to expand the geographic boundaries of Reconstruction northward and westward, the subject remains nestled contentedly within its domestic confines. Global histories of the nineteenth century often connect the Civil War and Reconstruction with contemporaneous struggles for national unification in Germany, Italy, or Japan. The comparative history of emancipation and race relations has improved our understanding of the U.S. experience. But the international context of America's Reconstruction era has more to offer.[2]

For a broader understanding of the post-1865 period, an obvious place to begin is with foreign relations and the projection of U.S. power and influence in the world. Historians have naturally paid great attention to Civil War–era diplomacy, but diplomatic histories of the Civil War usually end abruptly in April 1865. Treatments of post-1865 U.S. foreign relations have traditionally focused on Anglo-American relations and the *Alabama* claims, but only rarely have they turned to U.S. relations with other European powers or Latin America.[3] More often historians look forward to the war with Spain in 1898 and view the Reconstruction years as part of the long run-up to that fateful year of aggressive imperialism. In his iconic treatment of late-nineteenth-century foreign policy, Walter LaFeber folded the Civil War and Reconstruction eras into what he called the "years of preparation" for the imperialist turn in 1898. LaFeber and other followers of his mentor, William Appleman Williams, viewed America's imperialist impulse in 1898 not as an aberration but as the logical next step after antebellum U.S. continental expansion, the subjugation of the South, and the consolidation of power in the central government. Driving the "New Empire" was the relentless pursuit of new markets to absorb the rising productivity of America's industrial capitalist economy. William Seward, who served as secretary of state under Lincoln and Johnson (1861–69), has played a central role in this narrative as the chief architect of the new empire. An early champion of continental expansionism, after the Union secured consolidation at home, their argument goes, Seward pursued economic expansionism abroad.[4] What LaFeber and other historians mean when they refer to post–Civil War U.S. imperialism is not a "colonial empire," which Seward roundly denounced as unfitting to a republic, but instead a "commercial" empire and the expansion of a vast network of transportation, communication, and trade that was often facilitated by U.S. foreign policy and military. This informal commercial empire was certainly important to Seward's worldview, but his more immediate concern at the end of the war was protecting the United States from European powers that had proven antagonistic during the war.[5]

Our focus in this volume on the international context of Reconstruction, Latin America in particular, provides an ideal framework within which to examine the projection of U.S. power and influence in the world. This essay will deal with U.S. efforts to expel the French from Mexico, topple Maximilian's imperial regime, and restore the Mexican Republic led by Benito Juárez. The Mexican question was the foremost foreign relations problem the U.S. faced in the immediate postwar period. It also provides an illuminating case study of U.S. foreign policy in Latin America that differs from the conventional portrayal of Seward's nascent imperialist project.

Early in his political career Seward was an ardent advocate of expansion across the "American continent," an ominously elastic term that at times encompassed British and Russian possessions to the north, Mexico, Central America, the Caribbean, and even South America.[6] During his eight years as secretary of state (1861–69), Seward continued to voice Whiggish confidence in the inevitable spread of republican ideals and "institutions," but he typically envisioned this happening through the slow influence of migration and commercial and intellectual exchange, not by conquest and acquisition of territory.[7]

During the Civil War, Seward's most pressing goal was to thwart European powers from siding with the rebellion. He pursued this by a deft combination of hard-power threats against any who dared lend aid to the rebellion and soft-power appeals aimed at liberal opposition elements abroad urging them to stand by the Union as the beleaguered bastion of universal republican ideals.[8] After the war, Seward viewed the rapid reunification and consolidation of the wartorn United States into a powerful nation-state as the foremost goal of Reconstruction. Though he was consistently antislavery and deserves credit for pushing the Thirteenth Amendment through Congress, he harbored racist doubts about the capacity of black people and their readiness to participate in the life of the republic as full and equal citizens. These doubts and, perhaps more important, his determination to hold onto power as secretary of state and realize his postwar foreign policy aims led him to stand by President Johnson in his battle against the Radical Republicans.[9]

Seward's major foreign-policy achievement was the massive withdrawal of European empires from the Americas, particularly the French in neighboring Mexico. The idea that European imperial monarchies were inimical to republican institutions found useful employment in Seward's artful program of public diplomacy during the Civil War. After the war this idea took firm hold at home and in Latin America among those liberal leaders calling on the United States to uphold the Monroe Doctrine against European imperialist schemes to tyrannize American republics.[10] Consonant with this goal, near the end of his term as secretary of state Seward sought to acquire naval bases and coaling stations in the Caribbean and Pacific. The purpose in some instances was to facilitate future commercial expansion, but the more immediate concern was military defense, particularly in the Caribbean, which during the Civil War had served as a valuable launch site for European invasion, blockade-running, and Confederate raids on Union ships.[11]

The only territorial acquisitions made on Seward's watch, both occurring in 1867, were Alaska and a tiny, desolate Pacific atoll later known as Midway, which was, incidentally, seized without Seward's direction by U.S. Navy officers who thought it might be useful "especially in the event of a foreign war."[12] Several other opportunities to acquire territory presented themselves to Seward and his successor, Hamilton Fish, in Mexico, Cuba, San Domingo, and the Danish Virgin Islands, but they came to nothing for want of support in the State Department, Congress, or the public. The Alaska purchase would likely have met defeat had Seward not expedited matters so skillfully. Soon after the Alaska purchase, Seward explained his nation's waning interest in territorial expansion to George Yeaman, U.S. minister to Denmark, who was negotiating the sale of Denmark's Caribbean colonies to the United States. "The desire for the acquisition of foreign territory has sensibly abated" and the delays caused by Denmark "have contributed to still further alleviate the national desire for enlargement of territory. In short we have already come to value dollars more and dominion less."[13] In this last phrase, Seward neatly summarized the United States' turn from territorial to commercial expansion. At the end of a horrific civil war, facing the enormous travails of reconstructing the existing Union, it was no wonder that politicians and the public were unenthused about taking on more troubles trying to reconstruct distant lands and alien peoples. Underlying this apprehension toward expansion in Latin America were racial concerns that the United States should remain a "white man's country" and that the incorporation of dark-skinned peoples in tropical climates with languages other than English would be incompatible with the dominant Anglo-Saxon culture that many U.S. leaders deemed essential to prosperity and republican self-government.[14]

Under Seward, U.S. foreign policy aimed more at decolonizing neighboring territories than in acquiring them. During the Civil War the Union found itself surrounded by the appendages of European empires and slave regimes they believed were inimical to republican institutions. During the Civil War, as the Union struggled to dissuade Europe's Great Powers from siding with the Confederacy, those same powers took advantage of the situation by invading and conquering neighboring Latin American countries. Whatever European leaders thought about the Monroe Doctrine before 1860, they saw no danger in flouting it while the "dis-United States," as some delighted in calling it, were at war with one another.[15]

In March 1861, Spain swept into the Dominican Republic and took its former colony back into the empire. Led by a cadre of bellicose nationalists at home, the Spanish Empire proceeded to provoke wars with Peru and Chile, which many Latin Americans feared was part of an effort to re-colonize Spanish America. As the last European power still allowing slavery, Spain, though officially neutral in the Civil War, sympathized with the South's rebellion and welcomed its use of Havana as a port of call for blockade-runners and Confederate raiders carrying out piratical war against Union merchant ships.[16]

Britain also seemed ready to make the most of its former colonies' troubles. When a Union naval captain boarded the HMS *Trent* and apprehended Confederate envoys on their way to Europe, the British nearly went to war over this supposed affront to its flag. The government took the occasion to send ten thousand troops to Canada and bolster its fleet in the Caribbean.[17]

The boldest aggression in Latin America came from the French. According to Napoleon's "Grand Design," the control and stabilization of Mexico was the key to his plan for a canal that would cross Central America connecting the Atlantic and Pacific. Together with the French Suez Canal project, the Central American canal would realize the highest fulfillment of *Bonapartisme*, the revival of France's Napoleonic glory. According to French thinking on the subject, Mexico, like all the new Latin American republics, had degenerated because of the baleful influence of Anglo-Saxon culture emanating from the United States. The French mission as self-ordained leaders of the "Latin race" in the New and Old Worlds was to restore Mexico and eventually all Latin America to monarchical order and Catholic authority.[18]

The governments of Britain, France, and Spain had a deep stake in the outcome of the Civil War. Soon after the shots at Fort Sumter and before the war had even begun, each of these powers rushed to recognize the rebels as legitimate belligerents, a rebuke to the Union dictum that the "so-called Confederacy" was nothing more than a domestic insurrection in which foreign powers had no legitimate role. Britain and France repeatedly sought to mediate peace between the warring sections and on terms that would have effectively granted sovereignty to the South. Many in Europe continued to hope that the Union would exhaust itself and that the Peace Democrats would wrest power from the Republicans. The reelection of Lincoln and the collapse of the Confederacy in the spring of 1865 came as a surprise to many overseas. Southern sympathizers in Europe continued to hope Lincoln's assassination might reignite the South's will to fight for its independence. But their hopes came to naught, and Europe now confronted the victorious United States standing before the world as a nation at arms with over one million enlisted soldiers and legions of battle-ready veterans who had mustered out, plus a naval fleet exceeding seven hundred ships. It was arguably the most powerful armed force in the world.[19]

In the summer of 1862, General Juan Prim, commander of Spanish forces during the invasion of Mexico, had stopped in Washington on his way back to Spain. He visited President Lincoln and Secretary of State Seward, who invited him to review the Union troops commanded by General George McClellan during the Peninsular Campaign in summer 1862. Prim was astonished to see a massive citizen army, trained and disciplined, amply supplied with horses and mules, moving relentlessly through "immense woods" and able to cross deep rivers on quickly assembled pontoon bridges. Never mind that McClellan met disaster that summer, Prim was impressed with the army he had built. Theirs "was a work worthy of the Romans," he later wrote. "If the importance of nations is to be measured by the number of soldiers that they can put into the field, when these are well fed, armed, and equipped, the United States is the first nation of the world." When its war is over, Prim further warned, even if the South separates, "whenever the Monroe Doctrine is to be defended—America for Americans—they will form a single power, and woe unto those who shall dare to contend with them in America." Should this article, "perchance, come to the knowledge of the statesmen of France, it is to be hoped that they will take note of this prophecy."[20] Prim's ominous warning, echoed by opposition liberals in France, Spain, and Britain, slowly sank in by the end of the war. The Union had prevailed. A time of reckoning had arrived.

More was in play than the United States' military prowess and settling scores at war's end. Across Europe, tens of thousands of citizens were publicly demonstrating their solidarity with the United States by way of expressing condolences after the assassination of Lincoln. Suddenly, Lincoln became consecrated as an international martyr to liberty, emancipation, and, not least, to government of, by, and for the people—sentiments charged with danger for the aristocratic governing classes of Europe.

News of Lincoln's assassination arrived almost simultaneously with that of the Confederate surrender, and the response of the press and public was a mix of disbelief, emotional grief, and outrage. Everywhere, people gathered in the streets to learn the news. Some stood vigil for hours outside U.S. diplomatic posts, at first to confirm the truth of the reports and later to deliver messages of sympathy and solidarity. Once ridiculed in the European press as an example of the lowly material the democratic "mob" might elect to rule a nation, in death Lincoln suddenly ascended to that rare circle of international heroes whom any public figure insulted at their peril.

Across the British Isles, citizens of every social stratum, merchants and workers, women's reform societies and abolitionists, attended public assemblies in shire halls, churches, taverns, lecture halls, and grand amphitheaters to compose resolutions of condolence, some of them laced with criticism of the British government for not standing by Lincoln in his hour of need. Charles Francis Adams, the usually reticent U.S. minister to London, found himself thrust into the limelight in answer to all the manifestations of sympathy.

In France, where Napoleon III's Second Empire banned political meetings and speech, mourning Lincoln became a convenient excuse to stage demonstrations of sympathy and solidarity for *la Grande République*. Shortly after the news arrived, students gathered in the Latin Quarter preparing to march out the Champs-Élysées to the private home of John Bigelow, U.S. minister to France, when police tried to break up the gathering with swords drawn. Some escaped and made their way to deliver a heartfelt epistle of solidarity to Bigelow. Masons draped their lodges in black crepe, wore black armbands, staged funeral processions, and fired off mortuary salvos to honor Lincoln and defiantly display their republican sympathies. The liberal opposition in the Corps Législatif took the occasion of the Union's victory to glory in the success of a republic the imperialists thought dead. Eugène Pelletan, speaking for the opposition, rose to congratulate Lincoln, who "held the destinies of the New World in his hands, and he has shown himself equal to the emergency; he has abolished slavery, and he has founded a second time the glorious American republic." "Do not laugh," he rebuked hecklers, "you may be heard on the other side of the Atlantic."[21] In defiance of government censors, French opposition leaders sustained a campaign for over a year and a half, ostensibly to fund a gold medal for Mrs. Lincoln but also as a veiled political statement in favor of the republican opposition to Napoleon III's Second Empire.[22]

The response to Lincoln's assassination was especially poignant in Latin American. During the Civil War, republicans in Mexico, San Domingo, Peru, Chile and elsewhere implored Lincoln and Seward to protect them against the incursions of European empires, even proposing an alliance between the United States and the Spanish American republics to defend against aggression from France and Spain. They wanted nothing more than to see the United States uphold the Monroe Doctrine, which at that time Latin American liberals viewed not as a sinister vehicle for U.S. dominance so much as a welcome shield for all American republics against European aggression.[23]

From Cuba, the U.S. consul in Havana reported as early as January 1862 that Cubans "mingle with their songs the significant refrain 'Avanza Lincoln, Avanza, tu eres nuestra esperanza'" (Onward Lincoln, Onward, you are our hope). The "colored population are certainly somewhat agitated," another U.S. consul reported in October 1863; "the words 'Lincoln advances' are often heard in their songs and conversations among themselves." During the Civil War, Cuban slaves would "hasten to the wharves of the Island's capital and wait for news of the redeemer of [their] race." "In the decree of liberty for its Negroes," one Cuban later wrote, "the United States defined also the future of the Creole slaveowners."[24]

News of Lincoln's assassination caused "an unparalleled demonstration of grief" among Cubans, "especially among the Negroes." Men and women of all races wore black armbands with an image of Lincoln and "a device representing the American eagle," this in defiance of Spanish authorities who feared racial unrest and made certain that none of the many eulogies to Lincoln made any mention of him as *El Gran Emancipador*.[25] Young José Martí, only twelve years old at the time, remembered weeping for Lincoln, who became his lifelong hero.[26] Three years later, slaves responding to the call to arms in 1868 showed up brandishing images of Lincoln, anticipating that Cuba's revolution would vindicate Lincoln as liberty's martyr.[27] Portraits of Lincoln could also be found "in small modest rooms as well as in mansions which sheltered the high minded progressive leaders," one Cuban historian recorded, for Lincoln "became an expression of the high Cuban aspiration."[28]

Mexico's beleaguered republican leaders, forced into exile in Chihuahua, ordered flags to be lowered to half-mast and all civil and military employees to "clothe themselves in mourning during nine days." President Benito Juárez had learned of the Confederate surrender nearly a month after Appomattox and was stunned to learn of the death of Lincoln, he "who worked with so much earnestness and abnegation for the cause of nationality and freedom."[29] "The kindred people of this continent," a letter from a republican leader in Tabasco related on the Fourth of July, "united in the lovely bonds of democracy, ought to share mutually in its joys and its sorrows" and for this reason "Mexico will ever deplore . . . the death of the illustrious champion of liberty." Mexico, he promised, "will be a worthy member of the great democratic family that people the world of Columbus, in spite of the mean strategy now used to divide us."[30]

Chile did not learn of Lincoln's death until June 1, but the assassination might have happened that morning given the emotional impact it registered in Valparaíso. "The effect upon the residents of Santiago and Valparaiso was sad beyond description," Thomas Nelson, U.S. minister to Chile, told the home office. "Strong men wandered about the streets weeping like children, and foreigners, unable even to speak our language, manifested a grief almost as deep as our own." Nelson watched as Chilean citizens, "overcome by their emotion, sat down upon the very ground and wept; and men whose stoicism had never been affected gave violent course to their grief." Later they formed a procession and marched through the streets, as Nelson observed, "tears falling from the eyes of many, and the absolute silence and decorum of the thousands of spectators who filled the street."[31]

The explosion of demonstrations in favor of Lincoln and the condolence messages that poured into U.S. diplomatic posts abroad faded slowly during the summer of 1865, but the spirit ignited by the shared grief and outrage of that moment continued to resonate across the Atlantic. Dozens of books, speeches, and pamphlets appeared in the coming years, published in a variety of European languages, retelling the familiar story of Lincoln's rise from his humble origins as a woodsman to become the elected head of state. Never admitting any notion of Lincoln or the United States as being exceptional, foreign admirers instead embraced Lincoln as one of them, a universal symbol of how any democratic society might summon magnificent leaders from among its common citizenry.[32]

The most salient feature of the immediate postwar international scene was the massive withdrawal of European empires from the American hemisphere. Except for its assertive role in helping expel the French from Mexico, the United States did not dictate this retreat. Pressure came from within their colonial possessions, political opposition at home, rivalries in Europe, and the recalculation of imperial priorities. But the victory of the Union, its proven capacity for sustained war, and the display of popular sympathy toward the United States among European liberals certainly figured into the decisions Europeans made to evacuate the American hemisphere.

During the war, the United States found itself encircled by unfriendly if not hostile European empires encroaching upon vulnerable Latin American republics and posing the threat of allying with the South such that Seward feared any opposition from the United States would throw them into the welcoming arms of the Confederacy. Within weeks of the Union's victory Spain withdrew its occupation forces from San Domingo. In 1866, thanks to U.S. intervention as peace mediator, Spain effectively ended its shameful war against the allied republics of Peru, Chile, Ecuador, and Bolivia.[33] In Cuba, rebel republicans rose in arms in October 1868 and fought for ten years to end Spanish rule, but Spain would not let go of its "Pearl of the Antilles." Cuba's unfinished revolution would reignite in the 1890s.[34]

In the spring of 1867 Russia sold "Russian America" (later known as Alaska) to the United States, and in October it evacuated the North American continent. Russia was more concerned with defending a distant colony against British—more than U.S.—aggression, and Seward grabbed the opportunity to enhance the United States' window on the Asian Pacific.[35] Britain had long been concerned about potential U.S. aggression against its North American possessions, and the sale of Alaska—to say nothing of the annoying raids by Irish-American Fenians—did not help matters. Simultaneous with the Alaska purchase, Britain launched the Dominion of Canada in July 1867 as a self-governing, autonomous confederation and effectively withdrew from North America.[36] In March 1867 the last French troops left Mexico, leaving Maximilian and what was left of his imperial army to face the resurgent forces of Benito Juárez and the Republic of Mexico.[37]

The United States' role in expediting the expulsion of the French from Mexico and aiding Juárez's struggle to restore the Republic of Mexico illustrates many of the salient themes of postwar foreign policy under Seward. Because President Andrew Johnson (like Lincoln) lacked experience in diplomacy and quickly became embroiled in an impeachment crisis, Seward enjoyed an unusually strong hand in defining foreign-policy goals and strategies, which helps explain his loyalty to the beleaguered president. Seward's earlier reputation as an ardent expansionist and bellicose nationalist continued to hang over him as secretary of state. He remained ambitious for U.S. power and influence in the world, but his wartime experience as diplomat in chief brought a more mature view of the United States' place in the world. The bluster of an earlier time gave way to a confident conceit that the republican values and "habits of industry" the United States embodied would gradually take hold abroad, not by conquest and subjugation, which he thought contradictory to republican ideals and practically burdensome, but by an organic process of change through commerce and migration. In January 1866, during a private conversation with President Buenaventura Báez of the newly restored Dominican Republic, Seward gave a succinct summary of his foreign-policy goals. The United States had created a republic on a "broad foundation," an "imposing, possibly a majestic empire" that "requires outward buttresses." "To us," he continued, "it matters not of what race or lineage these republics shall be. They are necessary for our security against external forces, and, perhaps, for the security of our internal peace. We desire those buttresses to be multiplied, and strengthened, as fast as it can be done, without the exercise of fraud or force on our own part."[38] Seward's policy toward Mexico following the Civil War demonstrates this foreign-policy strategy.[39]

During the war, Monroe's 1823 declaration against any further European efforts to "colonize" the American hemisphere lay unenforced if not impotent because Seward feared that any effort to oppose European schemes in the Americas would throw France, Britain, or Spain into alliance with the Confederacy. After the war, as Juan Prim had warned, a victorious Union with a powerful army and navy stood ready to settle scores, and the French in Mexico were first on the list. During the latter stages of the Civil War there was loose talk of the Union and Confederate armies reuniting in a joint operation to oust the French from Mexico, an idea that found its way into the abortive peace talks at Hampton Roads in early February 1865.[40] The idea captured the imagination of European and Latin American liberals as well. Giuseppe Mazzini, the famed Italian nationalist, summoned the United States to lead a multinational "Universal Republican Alliance" whose first mission would be to destroy the "outpost of Caesarism" that France and Maximilian had imposed on Mexico.[41]

The French intervention in Mexico aroused new interest in the Monroe Doctrine, which, despite its wartime dormancy, quickly emerged as a central pillar of postwar U.S. foreign policy.[42] The doctrine also acquired new pro-republican ideological clothing as advocates began portraying it as a defensive shield for all American republics against the depredations of European monarchies. Aggressive actions by Spain against the Dominican Republic and by France against the Republic of Mexico gave ample proof of this Manichaean conflict between European imperialists and American republics. It should come as no surprise that among the stoutest advocates for the United States' standing up for the Monroe Doctrine were Latin American liberals who looked to the "Colossus of the North" as the defender of shared republican principles. What Mexico, the Caribbean, and South America were experiencing was not just random interventions, Peru's president wrote to the U.S. minister in Lima after the French invasion of Mexico, but "a war of the crowns against the Liberty caps."[43]

The new pro-republican iteration of the Monroe Doctrine also emerged out of the peculiar circumstances of the French intervention in Mexico. France insisted it was not colonizing Mexico and that Maximilian's empire represented the will of the Mexican people. At Maximilian's insistence, French occupation forces conducted a plebiscite in late 1863 to prove this very point.[44] Mexican republicans denounced the plebiscite as a charade, and their friends in the United States took the same view, but the French intervention presented friends of the Monroe Doctrine with a vexing case of regime change rather than European colonization. Their response was to redefine the violation as a European monarchist assault on American republicanism.

In April 1864, the month before Maximilian assumed the throne, both houses of Congress unanimously passed resolutions stating the United States shall not "acknowledge a monarchical government, erected on the ruins of any republican government in America, under the auspices of any European power."[45] Two months later, the Republican Party platform openly condemned "the attempt of any European Power to overthrow by force or to supplant by fraud the institutions of any Republican Government on the Western Continent." It further warned that the United States "will view with extreme jealousy, as menacing to the peace and independence of their own country, the efforts of any such power to obtain new footholds for Monarchical Government, sustained by foreign military force, in near proximity to the United States."[46]

One underlying assumption of this new elaboration of the Monroe Doctrine was that monarchical government by its very nature as a system of inherited dynastic power could never represent the will of the people.

More important, the imposition of a monarchy by "foreign bayonets" on any American republic endangered neighboring republics, not least the United States. Joshua Leavitt, a New England evangelical abolitionist who in 1863 wrote a powerful pamphlet elaborating the new pro-republican, anti-monarchical Monroe Doctrine, added a religious layer. The French plot against Mexico, he argued, was part of a larger conspiracy among the leading crowns of Europe, "sanctioned by the pope," against the "American republican system" of government.[47]

Few were more ardent in calling for armed invasion of Mexico by the United States than Matías Romero, the Republic of Mexico's young ambassador to the United States. During the U.S. Civil War, Romero, frustrated by Seward's timid hands-off policy toward the French intervention in Mexico, carried out a vigorous public diplomacy campaign to convince Unionists that there existed an integral link between the slaveholders' rebellion in the United States and the "Church party" rebellion in Mexico. Both were in rebellion against popularly elected republican governments. Both sought foreign intervention to defeat the popular will. Both, he warned ominously, must be crushed before either republic could live in peace. Romero built a powerful network by organizing dozens of Friends of Mexico clubs and enlisting politicians, journalists, and intellectuals to speak on the Mexico question at rallies and banquets at Delmonico's, a famous restaurant in New York City. At the end of the war, Romero helped organize a mass meeting at New York's Cooper Union that featured prominent speakers calling for the United States to stand by its "sister republic," Mexico, and defend the Monroe Doctrine for all American republics. The French invasion and the Southern rebellion, Romero told his audience, were "parts of one grand conspiracy." The sponsors of monarchical absolutism and human slavery "make common cause and strike a united blow against republican liberty on the American continent."[48]

Andrew Johnson would go down in history as the nemesis of black civil rights and Radical Reconstruction, but in foreign policy he championed intervention against the French in Mexico, a cause embraced by many Radicals. During the 1864 election, while Lincoln was distancing himself from the Mexico plank in the Republican Party platform, Johnson, his vice-presidential nominee, gave a full-throated endorsement of it during a speech in Nashville. "The time is not far distant when the rebellion will be put down, and then we will attend to this Mexican affair, and say to Louis Napoleon 'You cannot found a monarchy on this Continent.'" "An expedition into Mexico," he went further, "would be a sort of recreation to the brave soldiers who are now fighting the battles of the Union, and the French concern would be quickly wiped out."[49]

Romero naturally welcomed Johnson's advent to power, and one week after Lincoln's death he was delighted to learn that the new president was willing to meet with him. Romero handled the interview masterfully, flattering Johnson for his Nashville speech by telling him he had translated it and sent it to Juárez. As Romero laid out his thoughts on Mexico, Johnson "listened very attentively and without interrupting" except to ask questions about the military needs of the Mexican republican army. Romero came away satisfied that in Johnson Mexico finally had a U.S. president willing to act on the Monroe Doctrine.[50]

During the war, at his banquets, and through his Mexico clubs and publications, Romero constantly advanced the idea that the United States and Mexico were engaged in parallel and entangled struggles in defense of shared republican ideals. At war's end, he pressed the more practical point that the presence of the French and Maximilian next door posed an ongoing danger to the United States. On April 28, a week after meeting with Johnson, Romero invited to his home Ulysses S. Grant, the general in command of the entire the Union army. Romero had introduced himself a few weeks earlier by going to the front lines in Virginia. It was the beginning of a close, collaborative relationship. Grant was an ardent republican and a man who remained conscience-stricken by his role in the U.S. war against Mexico twenty years earlier, a war he considered "one of the most unjust ever waged by a stronger against a weaker nation." He judged it "an instance of a republic following the bad example of European monarchies."[51] Grant was furious over France's role in aiding the South, especially in Mexico, where the port of Matamoros, strategically located at the mouth of the Rio Grande, served as a backdoor to the Confederacy circumventing the Union naval blockade. Without Matamoros and the French, the South could never have sustained its rebellion.

It did not stop there, for in the spring of 1865 it appeared Maximilian was welcoming the defeated Confederates to make common cause with his regime. Jefferson Davis, still at large until May 10, was rumored to be heading to Mexico to rally his forces and carry on the war. Maximilian actively encouraged Confederate veterans to come to Mexico. William Gwin, a former senator from California and active proponent of the Confederacy in Europe, had fomented a plan to recruit thirty thousand Confederate immigrants to Sonora in northern Mexico, and he came to Maximilian with a letter of recommendation from Napoleon III.[52] In June, Maximilian named Matthew Fontaine Maury, an overseas envoy for the Confederacy, as head of the immigration project. Maury estimated that two hundred thousand southerners "had had enough of Republics" and would gladly cast their lot with Maximilian if offered proper "inducements." Among the inducements was an edict from Maximilian that allowed Southerners to bring slave labor into Mexico. More ominous in Grant's view, General Jo Shelby and a troop of some four hundred Confederate veterans crossed into Mexico to fight for Maximilian. Grant feared the enemy, defeated in the United States, was preparing to carry on a revanchist war against the United States from across the border. Not only would the Confederates in Mexico require the United States to maintain a large and expensive standing army on the frontier, which Grant viewed as inimical to republican government, but he also felt certain that it would lead to a much larger conflict in the future. Furthermore, he reasoned, the United States would never be more prepared to take on the French in Mexico.[53]

Grant and Romero began collaborating on what amounted to a clandestine military and diplomatic mission. Their plan was in blatant conflict with Seward's steady policy of neutrality toward Mexico, but it took form during a period when Seward lay incapacitated at home in Washington, D.C. A disastrous carriage accident on April 5 left Seward with multiple injuries, including a broken jaw and arm and a dislocated shoulder. Nine days later, the night Lincoln was shot, one of John Wilkes Booth's co-conspirators burst into the bedroom where Seward lay and lunged at the helpless invalid with a knife, slashing both sides of his throat and nearly severing his right cheek from his face. Seward recovered slowly, but he remained in extreme pain and was barely able to speak due to his facial wounds and a broken jaw, which required a heavy iron brace inserted into his mouth. The trauma of the assassination attempt, which left Seward's two sons seriously injured as well, took a tragic toll on Seward.[54]

Taking advantage of Seward's absence and Johnson's cooperative spirit,

Grant, working in collusion with the Mexican ambassador, effectively launched his own foreign-policy initiative, defining the Mexican question as a military threat that demanded a military solution. On May 17, 1865, he ordered General Phil Sheridan, who shared Grant's strong republican zeal, to go immediately to Texas and take command of some fifty thousand troops near the southwest border with Mexico. Sheridan was to crush whatever resistance he met from Confederate forces under General Kirby Smith, secure the border along the Rio Grande, and prevent Confederates from seeking refuge in Mexico.[55]

There was also a surreptitious understanding between the two generals that Sheridan was there to menace the French troops who were massing near the border and aid Juárez's republican army with arms and men.[56] To that end, Grant sent oblique instructions to Sheridan suggesting that he stockpile weapons and ammunition from surplus ordnance and "place them convenient to be permitted to go into Mexico if they can be got into the hands of the defenders of the only Government we recognize in that country." He further explained to Sheridan, "We want then to aid the Mexicans without giving cause of War between the United States and France. Between the would-be Empire of Maximilian and the United States all difficulty can easily be settled by observing the same sort of neutrality that has been observed towards United States for the last four years." Mexico needed men as well as arms. Grant instructed Sheridan to muster out men but let them keep their arms at 'low rates.'" "I will recommend in few days that you be directed to discharge all the men you think can be spared from the Dept. of Texas, where they are, giving transportation to their homes to all who desire to return. You are aware that existing orders permit discharged soldiers to retain their arms and accoutrements at low rates, fixed in orders?"[57]

By June, Grant and Romero had devised a scheme whereby one of Grant's most trusted officers during the war, General John M. Schofield, on official leave, would go to the border to conduct an "inspection tour" of U.S. forces along the Rio Grande. From there he would cross over into Mexico, taking any officers who wished to follow. They would enlist in the Mexican republican army, which would pay their salaries out of funds loaned by the United States to Mexico.[58]

Without knowing the details of this extraordinary scheme and no doubt aware of the growing popular enthusiasm for action on the Mexico question, President Johnson gave Grant free rein.[59] Romero was delighted. "Grant could not do more if he were a Mexican," he wrote to his superiors.[60]

On June 16, probably at Seward's suggestion, Grant was called to the White House to explain his plan for Mexico before the cabinet. Seward rose from his convalescence and made his painful way to the White House, a few doors away from his home, with a mind to expose and stop what he saw as Grant's dangerous game on the border. "The act of attempting to establish a Monarchy on this continent," Grant told the cabinet, "was an act of known hostility to the Government of the United States . . . and would not have been undertaken but for the great war which was raging, at the time and which it was supposed by all the great powers of Europe, except possibly Russia, would result in the dismemberment of the country and the overthrow of Republican institutions." The French-Mexican imperialists had violated all pretense of neutrality by allowing a plentiful stream of commerce through Matamoros to sustain the rebellion. Grant wanted to retaliate against France and Maximilian, but he was also concerned with the future military threat they posed. If the United States allowed Maximilian's regime to become firmly established, he warned, "I see nothing before United States but a long, expensive and bloody war; one in which the enemies of this country will be by joined by tens of thousands of disciplined soldiers embittered against their government by the experience of the last four years." "It will not do to remain quiet and theorize that by observing strict neutrality all foreign force will be compelled to leave Mexican soil. Rebel immigrants will go with arms in their hands. . . . [T]heir leaders will espouse the cause of the Empire, purely out of hostility to this government." "What I would propose would be a solemn protest against the establishment of a Monarchical Government in Mexico by the aid of foreign bayonetts." The Civil War, Grant told the president, Seward, and the rest of the cabinet, was not yet over.[61]

Seward sat through Grant's presentation, his ravaged face contorted by the iron brace that held his jaw in place. When Grant concluded, he adroitly answered the general's ambitious military plan, suggesting diplomacy and statecraft as the right solution for what he understood to be a diplomatic and political problem. First, he disarmed Grant by agreeing it was imperative that the French leave Mexico. But time was on our side, he insisted. Napoleon III would pull out of Mexico once he understood that the United States was never going to recognize Maximilian's regime and would never tolerate a European monarch imposed upon a neighboring country. Seward knew Napoleon was facing growing opposition from liberals at home, and much of their discontent centered on the disastrous Mexico venture. U.S. aggression in Mexico, he warned, would arouse French national pride, silence the French liberal opposition to his Mexico adventure, and force both France and the United States into a war that neither side could afford.[62]

Seward then raised another argument against military intervention: it might lead to a U.S. takeover of territory in northern Mexico. On this and several other occasions, the man supposed to be the pilot of U.S. imperial ambitions steered firmly away from territorial conquest. The "on to Mexico" enthusiasm among the U.S. press and public in 1865 was all too reminiscent of the spirit of southern filibusterism in the 1840s and 1850s, replete with promises of fabulous riches for the taking and loose talk of annexing northern Mexico's silver-mining district in Sonora. U.S. troops might invade Mexico to drive out the French, Seward warned, only to find "we could not get out ourselves." An army of liberation would become an army of conquest. Secretary of the Navy Gideon Welles watched Seward pick apart Grant's plan to the point that no support remained in the cabinet. That night Welles confided to his diary: "Seward acts from intelligence; Grant from impulse."[63]

Anyone alert to the boisterous popular enthusiasm for taking the war to Maximilian would have understood Seward's warning. Many Union veterans and a large segment of the American public seemed to have embraced Romero and Grant's idea that the Civil War was not yet over. In San Francisco the Monroe League staged banquets and torchlight parades to raise money and men for Mexico. The Defenders of the Monroe Doctrine, organized in New Orleans and Brownsville, Texas, and the Friends of Mexico Clubs, organized by Romero, all lent their enthusiasm to spreading information and arousing support for the Republic of Mexico.[64]

The passion for "on to Mexico" manifested itself in popular songs that appeared in 1865 and 1866. The song titles suggest the martial spirit of the day: "Get Out of Mexico!"; "Oh! I Vants to Go Home"; and "We'll Go with Grant Again." The final stanza of the last jingle gives some indication of the bravado:

There seems to be a little cloud just rising in the sky;
Napoleon, down in Mexico, is fighting rather shy
But Uncle Sam has let him know that he had better quit;
We're slow to take offence, my boys, but "mighty hard" to hit;
If Maximilian will not go, the way to fix him's plain,
We'll take the old familiar guns and go with Grant again.[65]

These and other popular expressions of Mexican fever coincided with recruitment efforts, some of which Mexico's republican government sponsored. Mexico paid former Union officers to recruit Civil War veterans, mostly Union, to go to Mexico, ostensibly as "emigrants" to avoid outright violation of U.S. neutrality. Colonel William H. Allen, a New York Union officer, employed as an agent of General Gonzales Ortega, a rival of Juárez for the presidency, organized the Mexican Emigration Company in May 1865 with offices and agents across the country. Promising bounties of $1,000 cash and 800 acres of land in Mexico, Allen boasted he had recruited 109,000 men by June 20.

The Emigration Company's advertisements combined inducements of wealth with the high-minded principle: "MEXICO, MAXIMILIAN AND MONROE DOCTRINE. All persons who desire joining a company soon starting 'to make a strike' for fame and fortune in the land of golden ores and luscious fruits."[66] Few of these "Crusaders for Saint Monroe," as the *New York Times* described them, made the trek to Mexico due to Ortega's perfidy and protests from France that these thinly disguised recruitment efforts violated U.S. neutrality. But the failed effort to mount an invasion was never due to any lack of enthusiasm among Union veterans to carry on the fight in Mexico.[67]

In San Francisco, Colonel George Mason Green, a veteran of both the Union and Mexican armies, led a more successful drive in May 1865 to recruit officers and men to fight in Mexico. Green's army was an elite corps of Union veterans who traveled more than ninety days by ship and horseback to northern Mexico. Juárez welcomed their arrival in Chihuahua and named Green's army the American Legion of Honor. The American Legion and other Union volunteers, many of whom were United States Colored Troops mustered out of Sheridan's army, made their way to Mexico to join the Juáristas.[68] The numbers of U.S. volunteers who fought were estimated at three thousand Union and two thousand Confederate veterans, most of the latter taking sides with the imperialists. The clandestine nature of their service and the distortions produced by national pride (U.S. and Mexican) make it difficult to assess the actual numbers of U.S. volunteers and their importance to Mexico's campaign against Maximilian. Whatever their numbers, the volunteers in Mexico lent credence to the popular idea of an international struggle between allied American republicans and European imperialists.[69]

U.S. volunteers joined a beleaguered republican army that in the summer and fall of 1865 was hard-pressed by the French army which concentrated its forces on Mexico's northern border in anticipation of a U.S. invasion. Sheridan despaired that the Republic of Mexico was about to succumb as Juárez and his government in exile withdrew from San Luis de Potosí, moving north to Chihuahua, and then in August 1865 to the U.S. border at Paso del Norte (today's Ciudad Juárez). Sheridan wanted to go in with twelve thousand U.S. troops, seize Matamoros, and clear out northern Mexico for the fraught Juáristas. Shelby and his troop of Confederate veterans had by this time joined the imperial forces along the border, Sheridan warned Grant, and numerous other prominent Confederates were entering Mexico with plans to colonize some of the richest portions of Mexico.[70] Seward's confident notion that time was on the side of Mexico's republic was not apparent to Sheridan, who witnessed Juárez and his republican army with their backs to the wall.

In September 1865 Sheridan mounted a hostile demonstration of force from the Texas side of the border. He reviewed U.S. troops stationed at San Antonio, as though to ready them for battle, then opened communications with Juárez asking questions about forage for his army and ordering pontoon boats to the Rio Grande. Rumors were "spreading like wildfire" that Sheridan and his army were about to cross over and join the republican cause. The French quickly withdrew from Matamoras and abandoned northern Mexico down to Monterrey. Juárez and his government returned to Chihuahua in November. The French retreat, Sheridan felt certain, presented a "golden opportunity" to rout the French and bring the war to an end. But Seward, responding to French diplomatic protests, issued strict orders against any "active sympathy" with the Mexican republicans. In his memoirs, Sheridan lacerated Seward's "slow and poky methods," which he blamed for another year and a half of bloodletting. At the end of 1865 the French struck back, seizing Chihuahua and forcing Juárez and his frail republican government to retreat a second time to Paso del Norte. From his precarious position on the border, Juárez waited to learn what the United States was going to do next about the French in Mexico.[71]

Meanwhile, Maximilian, under pressure from the French commanding officer, Marshal Bazaine, and hardcore Mexican conservative supporters, abandoned earlier efforts to reconcile with the Juáristas and moved toward rule by an iron hand. In early October Maximilian issued a stunning imperial edict known as the Black Decree. The emperor simply pronounced victory, claiming falsely that Juárez and the republican government "has left the country" and crossed into the United States. "From now on, the struggle will be between honorable men of the nation and bands of criminals and brigands. The time of indulgence has passed." Armed resistance to the empire would meet with summary executions. By his account, Maximilian intended only to terrorize the opposition, but his imperialist army slew tens of thousands of republican officers and men in service to his belated show of resolve.[72]

Seward's diplomatic solution may have been poky, but it was ultimately effective. Through John Bigelow, his able minister in Paris, Seward stepped up pressure for withdrawal, using all the demonstrations of public eagerness for war in Mexico, not least Grant's design, as reasons for France to consider a graceful exit and soon. Seward pounded the French and several other European governments with strongly worded protests against any efforts to sustain Maximilian's regime in Mexico and denounced Maximilian's collaboration with former Confederates to colonize Mexico and reintroduce slavery there.[73]

At the same time, Seward was determined to stymie Grant's plans for military intervention in Mexico. In July he met with General Schofield and persuaded him to postpone plans for Mexico and go instead to Paris as his special agent with a handsome budget and the able assistance of John Bigelow. His instructions were clear: "get your legs under Napoleon's mahogany, and tell him he must get out of Mexico."[74] What Seward planned for Schofield was the diplomatic complement to what Grant had Sheridan doing militarily—a demonstration for all to see that the United States was determined to get France out of Mexico.[75]

After agreeing to go to Paris, Schofield waited months before Seward finally issued his instructions in November. As a result, the long-anticipated arrival of the mysterious general in Paris in early December 1865 aroused tremendous interest in the Parisian press and set Napoleon's court at the Tuileries Palace abuzz with rumors about the prospect of war with the United States.[76] Schofield began his mission in Paris by attending the American Thanksgiving dinner at the Grand Hotel. The crowd and the Parisian press were eager to hear Schofield, who sat at the front table. A toast offered in his honor set off rousing applause while the band struck up "Yankee Doodle Dandy." In reply, Schofield spoke of the marvels of America's democracy at war. Among "the great lessons taught by the American war," he said to the hushed crowd, was that its government, though almost invisible in peace, in time of war quickly became "one of the strongest in the world [cheers], raising and maintaining armies and navies vaster than any ever before known [cheers]." No one could miss the warning. Schofield closed with a soothing toast to "the old friendship between France and the United States: may it be strengthened and perpetuated."[77]

News of President Johnson's first annual message to Congress arrived in Paris not long after Schofield arrived. Though it never directly mentioned the French intervention in Mexico, it included menacing language, drafted by Seward and intended to threaten war if the French did not withdraw. "We should regard it as a great calamity to ourselves, to the cause of good government, and to the peace of the world should any European power challenge the American people, as it were, to the defense of republicanism against foreign interference."[78]

Soon after Johnson's message arrived, Seward sent a strongly worded dispatch to Bigelow that amounted to an ultimatum. The United States desired to maintain its friendship with France, Seward instructed Bigelow to the tell the French, but this would be impossible unless France "desist[ed] from the prosecution of armed intervention in Mexico, to overthrow the domestic republican government existing there, and to establish upon its ruins the foreign monarchy which has been attempted to be inaugurated in the capital of that country."[79] News of the abrupt tone of Seward's December 16 dispatch alarmed Napoleon's court and helped the emperor understand the high stakes involved.[80]

Schofield continued his round of arranged meetings with close advisers to the emperor, including Prince Jerome Napoleon, the emperor's cousin who had publicly voiced objections to the Mexico policy, and Admiral Jurien de la Gravière, former naval commander of the Mexico expedition. Both counted themselves as friends of the United States and men who also enjoyed Napoleon's confidence sufficiently to convey Schofield's message that time was running out. Schofield never did get his "legs under Napoleon's mahogany"; they met only briefly at a formal reception and exchanged pleasantries. Seward and Bigelow had an understanding, it seemed, that as a diplomat Schofield made a fine general. His mission in Paris was to *not* be at Grant's disposal for some reckless venture in Mexico. But Seward also understood that the press attention to Schofield's activities in Paris and the rumors of imminent war with the United States that flowed through the network of Parisian gossip constituted exactly the kind of pressure the proud French emperor needed to focus his mind.[81]

On January 22, 1866, at his annual address to the Corps Législatif, Emperor Napoleon told the assembled political leaders that "in Mexico, the government founded by the will of the people is being consolidated; the non-contents [referring to Juárez and the republicans] vanquished and dispersed, have no longer any leader." None of this was true, but it allowed the emperor to honorably admit that the French expedition was *touche à son terme* (reaching its end), and that he was "coming to an understanding with the Emperor Maximilian for fixing the period for recalling our troops." The liberal opposition greeted this with loud cheers. Turning to the United States, the emperor expressed "sincere wishes for the prosperity of the great American Republic, and for the maintenance of amicable relations, now of nearly a century's duration." He alluded kindly to the French public's expressions of grief (and he might have added, protest) related to Lincoln's assassination, adding that "the emotion produced in the United States by the presence of the French army on the Mexican territory will subside before the frankness of my declarations."[82]

What Napoleon had in mind, it slowly became apparent, was a staged withdrawal of French forces from Mexico scheduled to finish in November 1867. The delayed withdrawal would only buy time for Maximilian to build an army and further entrench his government. Across the border in Texas, Sheridan increased pressure on the French during the first half of 1866 by continuing the covert shipments of arms, sending an estimated 30,000 guns from the Baton Rouge arsenal alone. Juárez's republican army won a series of stunning victories against the French and Maximilian's imperialist army. By mid-summer 1866, republicans had taken possession of the entire length of the Rio Grande and most of the territory down to San Luis Potosí. As the French retreated, rumors circulated that they might be pulling out ahead of schedule.[83]

In August 1866, in a desperate effort to rescue the Mexican empire, Maximilian's empress, Carlota, sailed to Europe to beg Napoleon III to stand by Maximilian. By the time she got to Paris, Carlota, by turns furious, pleading, paranoid, and hysterical, was rapidly falling apart under the strain of circumstances. Napoleon and Empress Eugénie gave her no comfort. Even as he met with her, Napoleon was deciding to move the final withdrawal of French troops ahead by eight months to March 1867. Napoleon sent a cable to Maximilian with the sad news: "We are in fact approaching a decisive moment for Mexico, and it is necessary for Your Majesty to come to a heroic resolution; the time for half-measures has gone by. . . . It is henceforward impossible for me to give Mexico another écu or another soldier." Carlota confirmed the verdict in her telegram to her husband: "Todo es inútil" (All is useless).[84]

Historians routinely describe Maximilian as a "puppet" of the French, but he was a puppet with his own mind, as Napoleon, Pope Pius IX, and the Mexican conservatives learned to their great chagrin, for he alienated the very parties essential to sustaining his throne.[85] Maximilian had fancied himself an enlightened, liberal monarch who would reunite Mexico's warring parties and bring the Juáristas into his government. For their part, the conservatives wanted nothing more than to wipe them out and be done with it.[86]

By early 1867, with French troops departing for Europe, Maximilian deluded himself into believing that his imperial army, along with remaining Austrian and Belgian troops, deserters from the French Foreign Legion, and volunteers among the Confederate veterans could defend his enfeebled empire against the republicans. Bazaine, the French commander, fearing some might blame him for Maximilian's demise, begged the emperor to abdicate and return with the French troops. Maximilian never fully believed that Juárez would execute a crowned European prince. Even as he faced execution during his last days, he hoped to escape and make his way back to Charlotte at Miramar, their home in Trieste.[87]

Soon after the French evacuation, Maximilian and a portion of his imperial army left Mexico City to take their stand at Querétaro, a more defensible position located 135 miles northwest of the capital. After a long siege, in May 1867 Querétaro fell to republican forces, and Maximilian surrendered without a fight. Republican officials put Maximilian on trial and quickly arrived at a verdict and sentence of death by firing squad. Humanitarian pleas to spare Maximilian's life came from all the crowned heads of Europe and even from leading republicans, including Victor Hugo and Giuseppe Garibaldi. Seward exerted all his diplomatic efforts to persuade Juárez not to execute the emperor. Even on the eve of the execution Seward appeared confident his life would be spared if only to prevent European retaliation.[88]

Juárez would have none of it. He could not afford to appear to be taking direction from the United States, for one thing. To pardon Maximilian and send him back to his Hapsburg family in Austria would only perpetuate the idea that he was the legitimate ruler of Mexico. In exile, surrounded by a loyal band of conservative Mexican supporters, he might think of returning to reclaim his throne. The first step of any European country with a grievance against Mexico, Romero explained, would be to intrigue with Maximilian and threaten to usurp the authority of its legal sovereign. To this point, it was telling that Maximilian's last decree was to appoint a regency of three men sworn to carry on the empire after his death.[89] Furthermore, the executions Maximilian carried out under his Black Decree left Juárez little choice but to exact revenge upon its author.[90]

News of Maximilian's execution on June 19, 1867, arrived in Paris precisely as Napoleon III was presiding over the opening ceremonies for the Universal Exposition in Paris (Fig. 7). The royalty of Europe and government heads from all the powers gathered in Paris, the gleaming capital of Napoleon's Second Empire, which Baron von Haussmann had renovated for the world to admire. The emperor made no mention of the execution, and for several days he banned the press from announcing it. The *Moniteur*, a government organ, denounced *les miserables* (the wretches) into whose hands Maximilian had fallen while valiantly defending his claim as legitimate sovereign of Mexico. French sensitivity on the demise of Maximilian lingered. The French artist Édouard Manet painted three enormous versions of the execution, but the government banned any showings, even disallowing lithographic prints of the paintings in public sight.[91] Echoes from the shots fired by Maximilian's firing squad rang mournfully across the Atlantic and over the grieving thrones of Europe that summer. They served as an ominous warning against further European designs on the American hemisphere.[92]

The shots fired at Querétaro also signaled the end of the two civil wars that had raged in North America for a full decade beginning with Mexico's War of the Reform. The Mexican republican army, it is obvious,

Figure 7. The execution of Maximilian and Generals Tomás Mejía and Miguel Miramón, who led Mexico's imperialist forces. The execution, on June 19, 1867, shocked the crowned heads of Europe and marked the demise of European imperialism in the American hemisphere. *Harper's Weekly*, August 10, 1867.

earned its victory over the French on the fields of battle, but in its hour of need the United States played an instrumental role in clearing the way to victory. To Seward goes credit for his astute application of diplomatic pressure in Paris, but that would not have sufficed had not Romero, Grant, and Sheridan advanced their clandestine scheme to aid the Juáristas with arms, men, and moral support.

Five years after the fall of Maximilian's empire, Seward and Juárez died within weeks of one another. Their passing presaged the demise of the spirit of republican camaraderie that had bound the two countries during their parallel struggles against reactionary rebellions. What followed in Mexico beginning in 1876 was the dictatorship of Porfirio Díaz, during which the Catholic Church resumed its conservative influence and foreign investors feasted on Mexico's resources. Simultaneously the United States retreated from the revolutionary promise of Radical Reconstruction and surrendered to a long reign of racial injustice in the South. In the often-troubled relationship between the United States and Mexico, the historical moment of friendship and common purpose that came at the end of the two civil wars served a cause worthy of both nations.

Notes

1. For more on the international context of Reconstruction, see Mark M. Smith, "The Past as a Foreign Country: Reconstruction, Inside and Out," in *Reconstructions: New Perspectives on the Postbellum United States*, ed. Thomas J. Brown (New York: Oxford University Press, 2008), 117–40. As Smith points out, Eric Foner's few pages on foreign relations "are the only pages in which a modern historian of Reconstruction inquires seriously into the broad significance, relevance, and meaning of foreign affairs to the period" (125). Eric Foner, *Reconstruction: America's Unfinished Revolution, 1863–1877* (New York: Harper and Row, 1988), 494–96. For recent efforts to internationalize the postwar era, see David Prior, ed., *Reconstruction in a Globalizing World* (New York: Fordham University Press, 2018); and Don H. Doyle, ed., *American Civil Wars: The United States, Latin America, Europe, and the Crisis of the 1860s* (Chapel Hill: University of North Carolina Press, 2017). For two exceptional efforts to integrate foreign affairs in the domestic narrative of Reconstruction narratives, see Mark W. Summers, *The Ordeal of the Reunion: A New History of Reconstruction* (Chapel Hill: University of North Carolina Press, 2014); and Steven Hahn, *A Nation without Borders: The United States and Its World in an Age of Civil Wars, 1830–1910* (New York: Viking, 2016).

2. Examples of global or Atlantic world treatments include C. A. Bayly, *The Birth of the Modern World, 1780–1914: Global Connections and Comparisons* (Malden, MA: Blackwell, 2004), 165; Jürgen Osterhammel, *The Transformation of the World a Global History of the Nineteenth Century*, trans. Patrick Camiller (Princeton: Princeton University Press, 2015), 449; Ian Tyrrell, *Transnational Nation: United States History in Global Perspective since 1789* (Basingstoke: Palgrave Macmillan, 2007), 89–93; Thomas Bender, *A Nation among Nations: America's Place in World History* (New York: Hill and Wang, 2006), 169–70, 177–81. Examples of scholarship on race and emancipation in comparative perspective include Peter Kolchin, "Comparative Perspectives on Emancipation in the U.S. South: Reconstruction, Radicalism, and Russia," *Journal of the Civil War Era* 2, no. 2 (2012): 203–32; Peter Kolchin, "Some Thoughts on Emancipation in Comparative Perspective: Russia and the United States South," *Slavery and Abolition* 11, no. 3 (June 1990): 351–67; Peter Kolchin, "The South and the World," *Journal of Southern History* 75, no. 3 (August 2009): 565–80; Eric Foner, *Nothing but Freedom: Emancipation and Its Legacy* (Baton Rouge: Louisiana State University Press, 1983); Steven Hahn, "Class and State in Postemancipation Societies: Southern Planters in Comparative Perspective," *American Historical Review* 95, no. 1 (1990): 75–98; Enrico Dal Lago, "The End of the 'Second Slavery' in the Confederate South and the Great Brigandage in Southern Italy: Some Comparative Suggestions," *Almanack*, no. 4 (December 2012): 63–74; Rebecca J. Scott, *Degrees of Freedom: Louisiana and Cuba after Slavery* (Cambridge: Harvard University Press, 2008); Frederick Cooper, Thomas C. Holt, and Rebecca J. Scott, eds., *Beyond Slavery: Explorations of Race, Labor, and Citizenship in Postemancipation Societies* (Chapel Hill: University of North Carolina Press, 2009); Thomas J. Pressly, "Reconstruction in

the Southern United States: A Comparative Perspective," *OAH Magazine of History* 4, no. 1 (1989): 14–33.

3. Among recent scholarship on U.S. foreign relations during Reconstruction are Phillip E. Myers, *Dissolving Tensions: Rapprochement and Resolution in British-American-Canadian Relations in the Treaty of Washington Era, 1865–1914* (Kent: Kent State University Press, 2015), and several works by Jay Sexton: *Debtor Diplomacy: Finance and American Foreign Relations in the Civil War Era, 1837–1873* (Oxford: Clarendon, 2005); "Toward a Synthesis of Foreign Relations in the Civil War Era, 1848–77," *American Nineteenth Century History* 5, no. 3 (2004): 50–73; "William H. Seward in the World," *Journal of the Civil War Era* 4, no. 3 (August 9, 2014): 398–430; "The United States, the Cuban Rebellion, and the Multilateral Initiative of 1875," *Diplomatic History* 30, no. 3 (June 2006): 335–65; *The Monroe Doctrine: Empire and Nation in Nineteenth-Century America* (New York: Hill and Wang, 2011); and "The Civil War and U.S. World Power," in Doyle, *American Civil Wars*, 15–33. See also Ian R. Tyrrell and Jay Sexton, eds., *Empire's Twin: U.S. Anti-imperialism from the Founding Era to the Age of Terrorism* (Ithaca: Cornell University Press, 2015), chap. 3.

4. Walter LaFeber, *The New Empire: An Interpretation of American Expansion, 1860–1898* (Ithaca: Cornell University Press, 1963), 1–39; see also Walter LaFeber, *The New Cambridge History of American Foreign Relations, 1865–1913* (Cambridge: Cambridge University Press, 2013), 1–19. On Seward's role as the architect of the new empire, see Ernest N. Paolino, *The Foundations of the American Empire: William Henry Seward and U.S. Foreign Policy* (Ithaca: Cornell University Press, 1973); and Richard H. Immerman, *Empire for Liberty: A History of American Imperialism from Benjamin Franklin to Paul Wolfowitz* (Princeton: Princeton University Press, 2012). For a more recent iteration of this theme, see Hahn, *A Nation without Borders*.

5. LaFeber, *The New Empire*, 60–61; Paolino, *The Foundations of the American Empire*.

6. Confusion continues to surround the concept of an "American continent." Many Europeans and Latin Americans refer to North and South America as one of six continents in the world. In the United States it is common to refer to North and South America as separate continents, increasing the number of continents to seven. Matters are further confused by the common Latin American appellation for U.S. inhabitants as North Americans (*norteamericanos*), though Mexico and Canada obviously share the continent. In this essay I avoid using "America" or "American" when referring solely to the United States except those few cases where the meaning is obvious and style demands variation.

7. Walter Stahr, *Seward: Lincoln's Indispensable Man* (New York: Simon and Schuster, 2012); Glyndon G. Van Deusen, *William Henry Seward* (New York: Oxford University Press, 1967).

8. Don H. Doyle, *The Cause of All Nations: An International History of the American Civil War* (New York: Basic Books, 2015).

9. Stahr, *Seward*, 417–18, 462.

10. Seward's thinking in some respects anticipated Cold War–era dichotomies of democracy versus Communist tyranny and, more recently, democratic peace theory, the neoconservative idea that democratic societies do not engage in war with one another.

11. Stahr, *Seward*, 454–57.

12. Stahr, *Seward*, 494.

13. Seward to Yeaman, September 28, 1867, quoted in *Memoir and Letters of Charles Sumner*, ed. Edward Lillie Pierce, vol. 4 (Boston: Roberts Brothers, 1893), 618.

14. Evidence of this thinking about race and climate is abundant in contemporary newspaper editorials and political speeches. For an excellent summary, see Eric T. Love, *Race over Empire: Racism and U.S. Imperialism, 1865–1900* (Chapel Hill: University of North Carolina Press, 2004).

15. Doyle, *The Cause of All Nations*, chap. 4.

16. James W. Cortada, "Spain and the American Civil War: Relations at Mid-Century, 1855–1868," *Transactions of the American Philosophical Society* 70, no. 4 (January 1, 1980): 1–121; Wayne H. Bowen, *Spain and the American Civil War* (Columbia: University of Missouri Press, 2011); Doyle, *The Cause of All Nations*, chap. 5.

17. Norman B. Ferris, *The Trent Affair: A Diplomatic Crisis* (Knoxville: University of Tennessee Press, 1977).

18. Alfred J. Hanna and Kathryn A. Hanna, *Napoleon III and Mexico: American Triumph over Monarchy* (Chapel Hill: University of North Carolina Press, 1971); Daniel Dawson, *The Mexican Adventure* (London: G. Bell and Sons, 1935).

19. Clayton R. Newell and Charles R. Shrader, *Of Duty Well and Faithfully Done: A History of the Regular Army in the Civil War* (Lincoln: University of Nebraska Press, 2011), 304; Nathan Miller, *The U.S. Navy: A History*, 3rd ed. (Annapolis, MD: Naval Institute Press, 1997), 114; "U.S. Military Manpower—1789 to 1997," http://www.alternatewars.com/BBOW/Stats/US_Mil_Manpower_1789-1997.htm.

20. Juan Prim y Prats, *General McClellan, and the Army of the Potomac* (New York: J. Bradburn, 1864); the Spanish version appeared in *La Iberia, Diario Liberal*, February 17, 1864.

21. *Foreign Relations of the United States*, 1865, 3:279–80.

22. Jason Emerson, "A Medal for Mrs. Lincoln," *Register of the Kentucky Historical Society* 109, no. 2 (2011): 187–205; Benjamin Gastineau, *La médaille de la liberté* (Paris: Librairie Internationale, 1865).

23. Sexton, *The Monroe Doctrine*, 85–122; Nathan L. Ferris, "The Relations of the United States with South America during the American Civil War," *Hispanic American Historical Review* 21, no. 1 (February 1941): 51–78.

24. Philip S. Foner, *A History of Cuba and Its Relations with the United States*, vol. 2 (New York: International Publishers, 1962), 131–35; Arthur F. Corwin, *Spain and the Abolition of Slavery in Cuba, 1817–1886* (Austin: University of Texas Press, 1967), 140; Dale T. Graden, *Disease, Resistance, and Lies: The Demise of the Transatlantic Slave Trade to Brazil and Cuba* (Baton Rouge: Louisiana State University Press, 2014), Kindle location, 4293.

25. P. S. Foner, *History of Cuba*, 2:133–34; Emeterio S. Santovenia, *Lincoln* (Buenos Aires: Editorial Americalee, 1948); Emeterio S. Santovenia, "Pasión cubana por Lincoln," *Revista de la Biblioteca Nacional Jose Martí*, no. 1 (1953): 59–72; Emeterio S. Santovenia, *Lincoln in Martí: A Cuban View of Abraham Lincoln*, trans. Donald F. Fogelquist (Chapel Hill: University of North Carolina Press, 1953).

26. P. S. Foner, *History of Cuba*, 2:133–35; Santovenia, *Lincoln in Martí*, 62–63; Santovenia, "Pasión cubana por Lincoln."

27. *Correspondence Between the Department of State and the United States Minister at Madrid and the Consular Representatives of the United States in the Island of Cuba, and Other Papers Relating to Cuban Affairs* (Washington, DC: Government Printing Office, 1870), 175.

28. Ramiro Guerra y Sánchez et al., *A History of the Cuban Nation*, vol. 4, *Break with the Mother Country (1837–1868)* (Havana: Editorial Historía de la Nación Cubana, 1952), 33; see also Adam I. P. Smith, "Land of Opportunity?" in *America Imagined*, ed. Axel Körner and Nicola Miller (New York: Palgrave Macmillan, 2016), 36.

29. U.S. Department of State, *The Assassination of Abraham Lincoln, Late President of the United States of America: And the Attempted Assassination of William H. Seward, Secretary of State, and Frederick W. Seward, Assistant Secretary, on the Evening of the 14th of April, 1865: Expressions of Condolence and Sympathy Inspired by These Events* (Washington, DC: Government Printing Office, 1867), 626–27.

30. U.S. Department of State, *Assassination of Abraham Lincoln*, 628–29.

31. U.S. Department of State, *Assassination of Abraham Lincoln*, 37–39.

32. Richard Carwardine and Jay Sexton, *The Global Lincoln* (New York: Oxford University Press, 2011).

33. Cortada, "Spain and the American Civil War," 39–40, 93–102.

34. Ada Ferrer, *Insurgent Cuba: Race, Nation, and Revolution, 1868–1898* (Chapel Hill: University of North Carolina Press, 1999); Ramiro Guerra y Sánchez, *Guerra de los diez años, 1868–1878* (Havana: Editorial de Ciencias Sociales, 1972); Antonio Carlo Napoleone Gallenga, *The Pearl of the Antilles* (London: Chapman and Hall, 1873).

35. Albert A. Woldman, *Lincoln and the Russians* (Cleveland: World Publishing Company, 1952); Norman E. Saul, *Distant Friends: The United States and Russia, 1763–1867* (Lawrence: University Press of Kansas, 1991).

36. Jacqueline D. Krikorian, Marcel Martel, and Adrian Shubert, eds., *Globalizing Confederation: Canada and the World in 1867* (Toronto: University of Toronto Press, 2017); Kenneth Bourne, *Britain and the Balance of Power in North America, 1815–1908* (Berkeley: University of California Press, 1967); Donald Creighton and Donald Wright, *The Road to Confederation: The Emergence of Canada, 1863–1867*, new ed. (Don Mills, Ontario: Oxford University Press, 2012); Phillip A. Buckner, *Canada and the British Empire* (New York: Oxford University Press, 2008); Christopher Moore, *1867: How the Fathers Made a Deal* (Toronto: McClelland & Stewart, 1997).

37. Hanna and Hanna, *Napoleon III and Mexico*; M. M. McAllen, *Maximilian and Carlota: Europe's Last Empire in Mexico* (San Antonio: Trinity University Press, 2014).

38. Frederick William Seward, *Seward at Washington as Senator and Secretary of State: A Memoir of His Life, with Selections from His Letters, 1861–1872* (New York: Derby and Miller, 1891), 310–11.

39. Joseph A. Fry, *Lincoln, Seward, and U.S. Foreign Relations in the Civil War Era* (Lexington: University Press of Kentucky, 2019), makes a convincing case for Seward's maturation as a diplomat following his famous "April Fool's Day Memorandum" of 1861.

40. William C. Harris, "The Hampton Roads Peace Conference: A Final Test of

Lincoln's Presidential Leadership," *Journal of the Abraham Lincoln Association* 21, no. 1 (Winter 2000): 30–61.

41. Joseph Rossi, *The Image of America in Mazzini's Writings* (Madison: University of Wisconsin Press, 1954), 137–48; Stefano Recchia and Nadia Urbinati, eds., *A Cosmopolitanism of Nations: Giuseppe Mazzini's Writings on Democracy, Nation Building, and International Relations* (Princeton: Princeton University Press, 2009), 219–23.

42. Sexton, *The Monroe Doctrine*, 123–24.

43. Robert W. Frazer, "Latin American Projects to Aid Mexico during the French Intervention," *Hispanic American Historical Review* 28, no. 3 (1948): 379. For overviews of the evolution of the Monroe Doctrine during the Civil War, see Dexter Perkins, *The Monroe Doctrine*, vol. 2, *1826–1867* (Baltimore: Johns Hopkins Press, 1933), 421–65; and Sexton, *The Monroe Doctrine*, 123–58.

44. McAllen, *Maximilian and Carlota*, 98, 108.

45. Perkins, *The Monroe Doctrine*, 2:451; Robert Ryal Miller, "Matías Romero: Mexican Minister to the United States during the Juarez-Maximilian Era," *Hispanic American Historical Review* 45, no. 2 (May 1, 1965): 232.

46. Republican Party Platform of 1864, June 7, 1864, Political Party Platforms, The American Presidency Project, University of California, Santa Barbara, http://www.presidency.ucsb.edu/ws/?pid=29621. Lincoln and Seward, fearing provocation of war with France, did not endorse this plank.

47. Joshua Leavitt, *The Monroe Doctrine* (New York: S. Tousey, 1863).

48. R. R. Miller, "Matías Romero"; Matías Romero, *Mexican Lobby: Matías Romero in Washington, 1861–1867*, ed. and trans. Thomas D. Schoonover (Lexington: University Press of Kentucky, 1986); Matías Romero, *Dinner to Señor Matias Romero, Envoy Extraordinary and Minister Plenipotentiary from Mexico, on the 29th of March, 1864* (New York, 1866); Matías Romero, *Proceedings of a Meeting of Citizens of New-York, to Express Sympathy and Respect for the Mexican Republican Exiles* (New York: John A. Gray and Green, 1865).

49. Perkins, *The Monroe Doctrine*, 2:471 n. 1; R. R. Miller, "Matías Romero," 2.

50. Matías Romero, *Correspondencia de la Legacion Mexicana en Washington durante la intervencion extranjera, 1860–1868*, vol. 5 (1865) (Mexico City: Imprenta del Gobierno, 1871), 259–61; for translated extracts from this correspondence, see Romero, *Mexican Lobby*, 50, 55–57.

51. Ulysses S. Grant, *Personal Memoirs of U. S. Grant*, vol. 1 (New York: C. L. Webster, 1885), 32.

52. Hanna and Hanna, *Napoleon III and Mexico*, xvii; for Grant's comments on Gwin, see Grant to Johnson, June 19, 1865, in U.S. War Department et al., *The War of the Rebellion: A Compilation of the Official Records of the Union and Confederate Armies* (Washington, DC: Government Printing Office, 1900), ser. 1, vol. 48, pt. 2:923 [hereafter cited as *Official Records*]; "European News," *New York Times*, March 26, 1865.

53. Andrew F. Rolle, *The Lost Cause: The Confederate Exodus to Mexico* (Norman: University of Oklahoma Press, 1965); Todd W. Wahlstrom, *Southern Exodus to Mexico: Migration across the Borderlands after the American Civil War* (Nebraska: University of Nebraska Press, 2015); George D. Harmon, "Confederate Migration to Mexico," *Hispanic*

American Historical Review 17, no. 4 (November 1, 1937): 458–87; Arthur Howard Noll, *General Kirby-Smith* (Sewanee, TN, ca. 1907), 250–55, 260–62; John N. Edwards, *Shelby's Expedition to Mexico: An Unwritten Leaf of the War* (Kansas City: Kansas City Times, 1872); Anthony Arthur, *General Jo Shelby's March* (Lincoln: University of Nebraska Press, 2012); Alfred J. Hanna and Kathryn Abbey Hanna, "The Immigration Movement of the Intervention and Empire as Seen through the Mexican Press," *Hispanic American Historical Review* 27, no. 2 (1947): 220–46.

54. Van Deusen, *Seward*, 411–16; Stahr, *Seward*, 431–32, 435–40.

55. Philip Henry Sheridan, *Personal Memoirs of P. H. Sheridan*, 2 vols. (New York: C. L. Webster, 1888), 2:205–29. Two historians estimate U.S. troops at 100,000: Robert Ryal Miller, "Arms across the Border: United States Aid to Juárez during the French Intervention in Mexico," *Transactions of the American Philosophical Society* 63, no. 6 (January 1, 1973): 15; and Robert B. Brown, "Guns over the Border: American Aid to the Juarez Government during the French Intervention" (PhD diss., University of Michigan, 1951), 231.

56. Sheridan, *Personal Memoirs*, 2:205–29; Ulysses S. Grant, *The Papers of Ulysses S. Grant*, ed. John Y. Simon, 31 vols. (Carbondale: Southern Illinois University Press, 1988), 15:213, 285–86, 367, 425.

57. Grant to Sheridan, July 25, 1865, in Grant, *Papers*, 15:285–86 (all spelling and grammar as in original).

58. Grant, *Papers*, 15:265; John McAllister Schofield, *Forty-Six Years in the Army* (New York: The Century Company, 1897), 379–80. The proposed loan from the United States opened the door to claims on Mexican territory as indemnity should Mexico default.

59. Grant, *Papers*, 15:285–86; Schofield, *Forty-Six Years in the Army*, 336–38.

60. R. R. Miller, "Arms across the Border," 15.

61. Romero's account of the meeting, as likely reported by Grant, is found in Romero, *Mexican Lobby*, 66–69; for Grant's written report of what he presented, see Grant to Johnson, June 19, 1865, Grant, *Papers*, 15:156–58.

62. John M. Schofield, "The Withdrawal of the French from Mexico: A Chapter of Secret History," *The Century Illustrated Monthly Magazine*, May 1897, 128–37.

63. Romero, *Mexican Lobby*, 66–69; Gideon Welles, *Diary of Gideon Welles*, vol. 2 (Boston: Houghton Mifflin, 1911), 317, quoted in Stahr, *Seward*, 444.

64. Michael Hogan, *Abraham Lincoln and Mexico: A History of Courage, Intrigue and Unlikely Friendships* (2016), Kindle location, 1807–1813.

65. George Cooper and Henry Tucker, "We'll Go with Grant Again" (New York: William A. Pond, 1866). The sheet music for songs related to the Mexico question are found in the Library of Congress's Civil War Sheet Music Collection, https://www.loc.gov/collections/civil-war-sheet-music.

66. R. R. Miller, "Arms across the Border," 34.

67. "Crusaders for Saint Monroe," *New York Times*, May 12, 1865; "Revival of Fillibustering," *New York Times*, May 9, 1865. On Ortega's claim to the presidency, see Ralph Roeder, *Juarez and His Mexico: A Biographical History* (New York: Viking Press, 1947), 611–14.

68. R. R. Miller, "Arms across the Border," 37–41; Robert Ryal Miller, "The American Legion of Honor in Mexico," *Pacific Historical Review* 30, no. 3 (1961): 229–41.

69. R. R. Miller, "Arms across the Border"; Brown, "Guns over the Border," 73–86; Lawrence Douglas Taylor Hanson, "Voluntarios extranjeros en los ejércitos liberales mexicanos, 1854–1867," *Historia Mexicana* 37, no. 2 (1987): 224.

70. Sheridan to Grant, August 1, 1865, *Official Records*, ser. 1, vol. 48, pt. 2:1147; for a full account of Sheridan's reports, see Sheridan, "Report of Operations of the United States Forces . . . in the Military Division of the South-West and Gulf and Department of the Gulf, . . . May 29, 1865, to November 4, 1866," in *Supplemental Report of the Joint Committee on the Conduct of the War . . . to Senate Report No. 142, 38th Congress, 2d Session*, 2 vols. (Washington, DC: Government Printing Office, 1866), 2:72–77.

71. Sheridan, *Personal Memoirs*, 2:215–17; Roeder, *Juarez and His Mexico*, 615–17.

72. Roeder, *Juarez and His Mexico*, 606–11; McAllen, *Maximilian and Carlota*, 207–8.

73. Because the United States did not recognize Maximilian's regime, Seward's protests went to France and other European governments, such as Belgium and Austria, involved in the intervention.

74. Schofield, *Forty-Six Years in the Army*, 339–40; Donald B. Connelly, *John M. Schofield and the Politics of Generalship* (Chapel Hill: University of North Carolina Press, 2006), 182–86.

75. Schofield, *Forty-Six Years in the Army*, 378–98; John Holladay Latané, *The United States and Latin America* (Garden City, NY: Doubleday, Page, 1920), 225–26; Connelly, *John M. Schofield*, 183–86; Perkins, *The Monroe Doctrine*, 2:474.

76. Schofield, *Forty-Six Years in the Army*, 385; Malakoff, "The Mystery of Gen. Schofield's Visit," *New York Times*, December 31, 1865.

77. Schofield, *Forty-Six Years in the Army*, 378–98, banquet toast on 386–87; Connelly, *John M. Schofield*, 183–86; Malakoff, "European Affairs . . . Thanksgiving Day at the French Capital," *New York Times*, December 24, 1865; Malakoff, "European News . . . How Thanksgiving Day Was Kept in Paris," *New York Times*, December 23, 1865.

78. "Andrew Johnson: First Annual Message," http://www.presidency.ucsb.edu/ws/index.php?pid=29506; Stahr, *Seward*, 445, 450–51.

79. *Foreign Relations of the United States*, 1865, 3:429.

80. Frank Edward Lally, *French Opposition to the Mexican Policy of the Second Empire* (Baltimore: Johns Hopkins Press, 1931), 111, 147, 159. Lally argues convincingly it was fear of war with the United States, not domestic and European concerns, that led to the French withdrawal, and he refutes Clyde Augustus Duniway, "Reasons for the Withdrawal of the French from Mexico," *Annual Report of the American Historical Association for the Year 1902* 1 (1903): 313–28.

81. Schofield, *Forty-Six Years in the Army*, 342–44; John Bigelow, *Retrospections of an Active Life: 1867–71* (New York: Doubleday, Page, 1913), 42. Seward's biographer drew on Bigelow's account to interpret the Schofield mission as a ruse: Frederic Bancroft, *The Life of William H. Seward*, vol. 2 (New York: Harper and Brothers, 1899), 435. For more convincing explanations, see Perkins, *The Monroe Doctrine*, 2:500–501; and Henry M. Wriston, *Executive Agents in American Foreign Relations* (Baltimore: Johns Hopkins University Press, 1929), 780–81.

82. "Full Report of the Emperor Napoleon's Speech," *New York Times*, February 8, 1866; Schofield, *Forty-Six Years in the Army*, 345; for diplomatic correspondence

surrounding the French decision, see Malakoff, "Three Days Later from Europe . . . France, Mexico and the United States," *New York Times*, February 16, 1866.

83. Sheridan, *Personal Memoirs*, 2:224–26.

84. Hanna and Hanna, *Napoleon III and Mexico*, 277–78; McAllen, *Maximilian and Carlota*, 273.

85. Erika Pani, "Juarez vs. Maximiliano: Mexico's Experiment with Monarchy," in Doyle, *American Civil Wars*, 167–84; Erika Pani, *El Segundo Imperio: Pasados de usos múltiples* (Mexico City: Centro de Investigación y Docencia Económicas: Fondo de Cultura Económica, 2004); Erika Pani, *Para mexicanizar el Segundo Imperio: El imaginario político de los imperialistas* (Mexico City: Colegio de México, 2001); Erika Pani, "Dreaming of a Mexican Empire: The Political Projects of the 'Imperialistas,'" *Hispanic American Historical Review* 82, no. 1 (2002): 1–31.

86. Jasper Godwin Ridley, *Maximilian and Juárez* (New York: Ticknor and Fields, 1992).

87. Seaton Schroeder, *The Fall of Maximilian's Empire: As Seen from a United States Gun-Boat* (New York: Putnam, 1887), 22–24; McAllen, *Maximilian and Carlota*, chap. 21.

88. Ridley, *Maximilian and Juárez*, 272–73; Schroeder, *The Fall of Maximilian's Empire*, 92–102; "Victor Hugo's Address to Juarez," *New York Times*, July 9, 1867.

89. Schroeder, *The Fall of Maximilian's Empire*, 94–95, 102n.

90. Ridley, *Maximilian and Juárez*, 228–40, 270; "The Fate of Maximilian: The Liberal Army Threatened Revolt If He Was Spared," *New York Times*, July 4, 1867.

91. "How the News of Maximilian's Death Is Received in Europe," *New York Times*, July 5, 1867; "Maximilian's Fate," *New York Times*, July 18, 1867; "European Intelligence: All European Courts in Mourning for Maximilian," *New York Times*, July 6, 1867; Alan Krell and Édouard Manet, *Manet and the Painters of Contemporary Life* (New York: Thames and Hudson, 1996), 87–91; John House, "Manet's Maximilian: History Painting, Censorship and Ambiguity," in *Manet: The Execution of Maximilian: Painting, Politics, and Censorship*, ed. Juliet Wilson-Bareau (London: National Gallery Publications, 1992), 87–111.

92. "Maximilian's Fate."

3

Jamaica's Morant Bay Rebellion and the Making of Radical Reconstruction

EDWARD B. RUGEMER

In the fall of 1865, as the states of the former Confederacy began to revise their state constitutions for re-admission to the Union, and as the new governments of the Old South passed the infamous Black Codes designed to maintain white power, a popular uprising in Morant Bay, Jamaica, dramatized with great violence the racial tensions that could persist in a slave society, almost thirty years after the abolition of slavery.

The uprising began with an altercation at the Morant Bay courthouse, triggered by a case of petty assault between two black teens. Protests against the fine of twelve shillings—the equivalent of five weeks' pay for a grown man—led to a small melee between the crowd and the parish magistrates, who blamed a man named Paul Bogle for stirring up dissent. Bogle was a prominent peasant leader and a preacher in the Native Baptist chapel at Stony Gut, a settlement in the hills about four miles from Morant Bay. The effort to arrest Bogle led to several days of violence in Morant Bay and on at least twenty nearby sugar plantations. When it was over, eighteen white men lay dead, and more had been wounded. As fear and paranoia swept through the island's small white population, Governor Edward Eyre in Spanish Town declared martial law and mobilized troops to put down the violence. In the following weeks the forces of Great Britain killed almost five hundred people, left hundreds more badly wounded from brutal floggings, and destroyed the homes of a thousand peasant families, the first generation of black Jamaicans born into freedom.

The shocking disproportion in the violent response of the colonial state drew widespread attention in Great Britain and in the United States.

Coming in the midst of Presidential Reconstruction, and almost thirty years after the abolition of West Indian slavery, the Morant Bay Rebellion dramatized one result of an emancipation process thirty years in the making. For American observers on the very cusp of their nation's own process of emancipation, Morant Bay served as a warning of what might take place in the American South.[1]

Before we begin this history, it is important to establish two premises about the law upon which the argument of this essay rests. The first is that the policy goals of Radical Reconstruction can be understood through a careful reading of two acts passed by the U.S. government in 1866 and 1867, namely, the Civil Rights Act of 1866 and the First Reconstruction Act of 1867. The second is that I largely accept Jürgen Habermas's description of how lawmaking works in democratic practice. In his 1996 work *Between Facts and Norms*, Habermas described periods of "opinion formation" and "will formation" that shape the governance of democratic societies. Opinion formation takes place in the chaotic public sphere. It is a historical process through which public opinion, or better yet, multiple public opinions, form about a given political issue. Will formation follows the development of public opinion and takes place within government, whereby legislatures, courts, and executive powers establish laws and policies that attempt to manifest that public opinion.[2]

The central political questions in the United States in 1865 and 1866 revolved around federal policy toward the former Confederate states. Perhaps most significantly, the question of what the federal government should do, if anything, to ensure the "freedom" of those who had been enslaved became the topic of extended discussion in the press and ultimately in Congress. The Reconstruction legislation of 1866 and 1867 represented a moment of will formation when the Radical Republicans who controlled the Congress established a legal framework for the process of emancipation in the American South as they imagined it would unfold.

Public opinions about these questions were shaped by the vibrant and boisterous newspaper press of the nineteenth century, which, as Mark Summers has recently shown, published rumor, "fake news," and highly partisan writing. The Radical Republicans who wrote the historic legislation of the Thirty-Ninth Congress were steeped in this journalism. The war had enabled these men to accomplish one major policy goal—the abolition of slavery. The war had also destroyed much of the land and killed nearly a million people. These epochal events, along with alarming developments in the former Confederacy, such as severe episodes of racial violence and the election of former Confederates to high positions, were no doubt primary in the minds of the members of Thirty-Ninth Congress. But we must also consider the role of events elsewhere in the Atlantic world that, because of their drama and immediate significance, attracted the attention of American newspaper editors, who shared these stories with their readers.

In the effort to internationalize our understanding of Reconstruction, it is critical that we recognize that the process of emancipation which began in the American South during the Civil War had already unfolded numerous times under a variety of political circumstances in other regions of the Atlantic world. Racial slavery had been foundational to the development of an Atlantic world since the sixteenth century, yet beginning in the 1780s the abolition of slavery transformed the northern United States, the French colony of Saint Domingue (which in 1804 became Haiti), most of Spanish America, and the Caribbean colonies of Britain, France, the Netherlands, and Denmark. The transformation of a slave society into a society without slavery had taken place several times by the eve of America's Civil War, and political writers had offered considerable commentary on the meaning of those emancipations. Because trade and the circulation of information closely connected the societies of the Atlantic world, the abolition of slavery not only initiated a sociopolitical process on the ground that transformed emancipated societies but also generated an intellectual discourse that drew meaning from previous experiences of abolition. Atlantic societies stood in very different moments of historical time with respect to the abolition of slavery, but their entangled public spheres allow historians to formulate an Atlantic history of slavery's abolition that recognizes both the distinctions of political context and the cumulative dimensions of slavery's demise. The internationalization of the Reconstruction era makes an important contribution to this widened stream of modern historiography.[3]

Jamaica and the American South saw two distinct processes of emancipation, but from the fall of 1865 to the spring of 1867 these emancipations intersected through the international impact of the Civil War and through the operation of the transatlantic public sphere of newspapers. American understandings of the process of emancipation in Jamaica had percolated for almost thirty years before secession, which made the events of the

Morant Bay Rebellion highly relevant to the process of opinion formation in the United States before and during the momentous legislative sessions of the Thirty-Ninth Congress. Many factors—local, national, and international—shaped the making of Radical Reconstruction: Jamaica's Morant Bay Rebellion of 1865 was one of them.

Almost thirty years before the Civil War, the convergence of organized slave resistance and abolitionist agitation brought the destruction of slavery to Great Britain's Caribbean empire. As Britain's largest and most productive sugar colony, Jamaica played an outsized role in the contentious history of the British Caribbean in the early nineteenth century. Absentee planters from Jamaica such as Bryan Edwards, William Beckford, and Stephen Fuller were among the most prominent West Indians in London during the 1780s when British abolitionism began to take root. These men led the West Indian interest, which had lobbied for the sugar islands since the seventeenth century and now sought to obstruct abolitionist efforts to cleanse the British Empire of the moral stain of racial slavery. Their efforts were largely successful until 1807, when British abolitionists pushed through Parliament the legislation that would abolish Britain's participation in the transatlantic slave trade.[4]

Within months of Parliament's passage of the Act of Abolition, the U.S. Congress prohibited American participation in the transatlantic slave trade. Such proximity in time should not obscure the distinct historical processes at work in two very different political contexts. The international dimensions of the rise and fall of racial slavery were intrinsic to the way contemporaries understood these developments during most of the nineteenth century.

In the United States, slave-trade abolition fulfilled an aspiration of the founding generation written into one of the many compromises of the Constitution. Antislavery delegates from Virginia and the Mid-Atlantic states had wanted the new constitution to abolish the trade, but delegates from South Carolina were adamant in their opposition to such a ban. The South Carolinians had support from some of the New England delegates who represented ports where transatlantic slavers still operated. Antislavery ideas and economic interests worked in tandem in the U.S. context. Slaveholders in Virginia and New York saw the market opportunities in the domestic slave trade that some Pennsylvania slaveholders had begun to exploit. But the planters of South Carolina and Georgia wanted to be able to important enslaved Africans at the lower prices offered by the transatlantic slave trade. And the South Carolina delegates severely resented the implication that slavery was somehow morally wrong. The result of these stark disagreements was a clause in the Constitution that postponed consideration of the abolition of the slave trade for twenty years after ratification. When that moment arrived, the Virginian Thomas Jefferson was president and his Democratic Republicans successfully pushed through legislation to abolish the trade, over the protests of the delegations from Georgia and South Carolina.[5]

In Great Britain, slave-trade abolition resulted from the work of an organized abolitionist movement intimately connected with prominent British politicians, who with great dexterity manipulated the politics of national identity to advance abolitionism during years of war with Napoleonic France. Parliament's first anti-slave-trade law served as a wartime measure that targeted the colonial interests of Britain's rivals. The Foreign Slave Trade Act of 1806 prohibited Britain's transatlantic slavers from trading with any of the colonies Britain had just seized from France, as well as the colonies of any foreign power. The law especially targeted the British slave trade to Cuba, Jamaica's principal economic rival, which since 1802 had launched sixty-one slaving voyages from West Africa to the Spanish colony, bringing more than thirty thousand people from the lands of their birth to labor in the Spanish island's flourishing sugar industry. In the months following the passage of this law, abolitionists worked to influence Britain's parliamentary elections by demanding and publicizing candidate positions on the abolition of the slave trade. The election brought into Parliament a majority of members willing to support abolition, and in 1807 Parliament passed the Act for the Abolition of the Slave Trade, which prohibited its merchants from engaging in this profitable commerce that had occupied Britons since the sixteenth century.[6]

The British and American abolitions of the transatlantic slave trade may have been similar legal actions, but each abolition flowed from its particular history, and the impact of abolition would be very different in the United States and Great Britain. In the United States, the abolition of the transatlantic slave trade actually deepened the commitment of American slaveholders to defending slavery during the tumultuous era that followed the Haitian Revolution. Cotton production in the Deep South was in the midst of its own astonishing transformation, which created an enormous market demand for enslaved African American laborers. The intensification of cotton production accompanied a more gradual economic shift in Maryland and Virginia toward an increasingly mixed agriculture less dependent on enslaved labor. American slave traders opened a domestic trade that forcibly relocated thousands of young men and women from the slave communities of Virginia and Maryland to the cotton frontiers that opened up in Alabama, Mississippi, and Louisiana. This economic foundation for slavery strengthened the proslavery resolve of American slaveholders, lessening sectional disagreements about slavery among the regions of the slaveholding South. In such a national context, there was no reason to believe that the abolition of America's transatlantic slave trade might lead to the abolition of American slavery itself.[7]

The history of abolitionism in Great Britain and its Caribbean empire could not have been more different. British abolitionists emerged from their victory over the transatlantic slave trade with a considerable bank of moral capital. Some abolitionists hoped that the abolition of the slave trade would compel slaveholders to reform slavery itself, but others believed that slavery itself was as morally criminal as the slave trade. In 1815, when British abolitionists learned that West Indian planters sought to import African captives despite the ban, they again mobilized popular support behind a Slave Registration Act that would monitor West Indian compliance with slave trade abolition. Historians have not found much evidence of a fraudulent slave trade to the West Indies after the British ban, but abolitionist agitation fostered the emergence in Great Britain of a significant antislavery constituency, a public opinion that would have a profound impact on the politics of slavery. In stark contrast, American abolitionism consisted of a small, interracial group of dedicated activists who had very little public following and less influence in Congress. American abolitionism would develop and grow, but only after British abolitionists had successfully pushed through legislation that abolished slaveholding throughout Britain's Caribbean colonies.[8]

Organized slave resistance in the Caribbean played an equally critical role to Britain's abolition of colonial slavery in 1833. Scholars have shown that as abolitionist agitation in the metropole intensified from 1815 to 1832, slave rebels took advantage of the political crises that abolitionism posed to slaveholders, and launched the most significant slave rebellions that Britain's Caribbean colonies had ever seen. When Britain's abolitionists accomplished some small victory in London, the response among the West Indian elite could be strident and public in opposition to a Parliament acting in the interests of the people they enslaved. Rumors spread among the enslaved that colonial slaveholders obstructed abolitionist efforts to establish wages for sugar work, to distribute land, or even to abolish slavery altogether. Rumors fostered the organization of conspiracies that launched major rebellions in Barbados in 1816, in Demerara in 1823, and in Jamaica in 1831. The rebellion of Jamaica's slaves would be the single largest slave insurrection in the history of the British Caribbean. The rebellion followed closely upon a huge effort among British abolitionists to push Parliament toward the immediate abolition of colonial slavery. Abolitionists had staged mass public meetings and flooded Parliament with more than five thousand petitions from disparate communities of the United Kingdom, demanding that Parliament enact legislation to abolish slavery immediately.[9]

Most West Indian planters were outraged, and according to some accounts, rebel leaders in Jamaica organized the enslaved response as a massive labor strike to begin after the Christmas holidays, when all were supposed to resume labor. But other rebel leaders planned a more forceful response to the slaveholder intransigence. This group organized a rebellion that spread through half of the island. Rebellion led to reaction. Jamaica's governor mobilized regular troops from the colony's garrison, who fought alongside the colonial militia and two companies of treaty Maroons to suppress the rebellion. The rebels killed fourteen white men, but Jamaica's colonial forces killed more than three hundred in the field during the suppression of the rebellion, and in its aftermath, the colonial state executed 344 men and women, accused of rebellion, in courts-martial that filled the gallows of Montego Bay.[10]

The white reaction in Jamaica targeted not only the enslaved but also the sectarian missionaries, mostly Baptists and Methodists. Present in the island since the 1780s, these missionaries had established Christian communities among the slaves, and some enslaved members of the mission churches were deeply involved with the rebellion. Samuel Sharpe, whom colonial whites accused of being the principal leader among the rebels, was a prominent deacon in the Baptist mission in Montego Bay led by the English missionary Thomas Burchell. Some have argued that Sharpe used his position among the Baptists to organize the labor strike, but clearly, Sharpe did not possess enough authority to control the rebellion. Sharpe's actual role notwithstanding, local whites mobbed Burchell when he arrived in Montego Bay during the rebellion, and throughout the island more than a dozen sectarian chapels were torn down by white mobs. One white mob tarred and feathered the missionary Henry Bleby.

Such news had great impact upon the growing antislavery constituency of Great Britain. Prominent and well-respected abolitionists such as William Wilberforce had long argued that slavery was morally wrong and a stain upon Britain's national character. The actions of Jamaica's whites proved this point with great drama, as colonial slaveholders tortured men of God and tore down their places of worship. Covered extensively by metropolitan newspapers, the story of the rebellion and its aftermath shaped public opinion in the UK during a critical moment. The Reform Bill of 1832 passed while news from Jamaica still resonated. Britain's abolitionists capitalized on the public's scorn for slavery by demanding that candidates for office pledge to vote for immediate abolition. These political efforts were successful, and when abolitionist parliamentary leaders introduced a bill to abolish colonial slavery in August 1833, they finally had the votes to get it passed.[11]

Great Britain's Slavery Abolition Act was a radical measure implemented along rigidly conservative lines. The law eliminated a long-established form of private property, the capital investment in slaves, but it did not require protections for the human rights of the people being freed. Parliament distributed £20,000 compensation for the capital losses sustained by slaveholders in the colonies, as well as absentee investors in slave property resident in the UK. Land remained the legal property of the men and women who owned it at the moment of abolition. Most landowners in the colonies, of course, had been slaveholders, and the lands they held had been developed and improved by generations of captive Africans and their descendants. The law allowed no land for distribution among those freed.

With respect to labor, the abolition law compelled former slaves to work for their previous masters for forty hours per week without pay for a term of four to six years—four years for women domestics and men skilled in a trade, and six for common field workers. Those once enslaved would continue to receive the food rations they had as slaves, and they would be able to maintain the provision grounds they had worked as slaves and to remain in the homes they had built when enslaved. But at the moment of emancipation their old masters would certainly have reminded them that the land they lived on and worked in, the land where their fathers and mothers were buried, still belonged to the master. As the former Confederate general Robert Richardson said regarding the freedpeople of the American South, the abolition of slavery in the British Caribbean offered "nothing but freedom" to those who had been enslaved.[12]

By the eve of the American Civil War, most black Jamaicans were very poor, most could not read, most could not vote, and many had become aggrieved. Free from slavery for almost thirty years, some had become the backbone of a hardworking peasantry with their own small, freehold properties. But many more remained dependent for work upon the sugar plantations. Jamaica had been one of the British Empire's most profitable colonies in the eighteenth century, but its sugar industry had been in decline since the abolition of the transatlantic slave trade. Since the abolition of slavery itself, sugar production had fallen by more than half. Most Jamaican peasants still worked for the plantations, if only seasonally, but many had established their own freehold properties. They grew food for the local markets, as well as crops such as allspice and bananas for export. Independent peasants would still work for the sugar planters, but only on their own terms, and Jamaica's sugar planters faced steep competition from Cuba and Brazil, the most powerful sugar industries of the Second Slavery, which, like the American South, still depended on chattel slavery. Abolitionists in Parliament had once protected Britain's sugar islands with preferential tariffs in the home market, but these had fallen to the new orthodoxy of free trade in 1846. When the tariffs fell the price of sugar fell, and most of Jamaica's plantations would only pay low and irregular wages on a seasonal basis.[13]

In an effort to maintain their wealth and status, the island's planter elite had used its political power to bolster the plantations and to shift the cost of governance onto the peasantry. The Jamaica Assembly had sponsored immigration schemes to bring to the island indentured laborers from Africa and South Asia. Such workers were cheaper for the planters, and their presence kept wages down. The assembly structured the tax code to favor the planters as well, and to impede the peasant's progress. A farmer's cart, for example, was taxed at 18 shillings per year; the same cart used on a plantation was not taxed.[14]

Jamaican law denied the vote to people of African descent not explicitly by race, but through a measure of property. Only freeholders or successful artisans could qualify and while their numbers were significant, during the assembly elections of 1864 only 1,903 Jamaicans voted, less than one-half of one percent of a population of 440,000. Some of these voters were black men, but more were known as "browns"—descendants of the slave society's free people of color. Even more voters were white men, who represented 3 percent of the island's population. White men still held most positions of colonial authority, but black and brown men had secured positions in the local vestry governments and had even won seats in the prestigious Colonial Assembly, an institution more than two hundred years old. Black and brown politicians often coordinated with Jewish men, who had also been denied political inclusion in Jamaica until 1830. Blacks, browns, and Jews were the only members of the political elite who sometimes advocated for the interests of the black peasantry.[15]

Baptists, who remained devoted abolitionists, were among the first to sound the alarm that the process of emancipation in Jamaica had gone very wrong. In 1859, Edward Underhill, secretary of the Baptist Missionary Society, visited the Caribbean and, three years later, published *The West Indies: Their Social and Religious Condition*. Underhill described the poverty of the people, their difficulty in finding work, and conflicts over wages between laborers and planters. Churches maintained the island's only schools, and most of their students were white and brown. Black children, by far the majority, received no schooling at all. Despite these obstacles the Baptist missions had persevered, and Underhill closed his account of Jamaica on a positive note, expressing his certainty that a "trustworthy middle class [was] rapidly forming."[16]

But in the years following publication of his book, Underhill learned from correspondents in Jamaica that conditions had become much worse. There had been drought followed by floods, which destroyed crops, and the Union blockade of Confederate ports had cut off much of the trade with the United States. The prices of necessary imports such as food and clothing increased dramatically at a time when many peasants were often out of work. Some turned to theft in order to survive, and so violence increased as the cycle of theft and retribution intensified.

In January 1865, Underhill wrote privately to the secretary of state for the colonies, Edward Cardwell, a family friend. The pastor described the hardships people faced in Jamaica, but he went further and laid the blame for such conditions upon colonial policy and its blind support of the sugar planters. Underhill wrote that the colony must respond to the needs of the black majority, who had, after slavery, proven their ability to thrive but lacked the capital and the land to prosper.[17]

Cardwell forwarded the letter to Governor Eyre, who believed it to be nonsense and sent it around the island to his political allies, most of whom were sugar planters. The third son of an Anglican rector in the East Riding of Yorkshire, England, Eyre had been made lieutenant governor of Jamaica in 1862 during the illness of his predecessor. Eyre was a man of empire for most of his adult life. His older brothers had died very young and Eyre's father had saved £400 with the hopes that his surviving son might buy a commission in the army. But the young man took the money and went to Australia instead, where he prospered as a sheepherder and was eventually appointed "Protector of the Aborigines." A successful career in imperial governance followed with appointments to New Zealand, St. Vincent's, and finally Jamaica. Eyre quickly made alliances among the leading planters but found himself in frequent conflict with one George William Gordon, a brown man who identified with and represented the interests of the black peasants of his parish, St. Thomas in the East.[18]

The circulation of Underhill's letter and vigorous debate in the Jamaican press created the atmosphere for a series of public meetings throughout the island from April until late June of 1865. The Underhill meetings, as they came to be known, gave voice to the immense frustration among the black majority; the brown and black politicians who represented the black peasantry organized many of these meetings. These public meetings, which were also described in the local press, affirmed Underhill's assessment of the situation on the island, but many went further in demanding that Crown lands be made available for purchase or rent at rates that were affordable to small-holders. One contemporary estimated that the Crown possessed almost nine hundred thousand acres of former plantation land, forfeited to the Crown for the failure to pay quitrents. Critics of the colonial government believed this land should be used to aid the island's poor majority, the black peasantry not two generations from slavery. The meetings were well publicized and covered in the Jamaican press, but American newspapers did not yet devote space to the news from Jamaica. Understandably, Americans were still reeling from the assassination of Abraham Lincoln.[19]

The official response to the petitions that came from the Underhill meetings came to be known as the "Queen's Advice." It was in fact a memorandum written by Henry Taylor, the colonial official who had been one of the main architects of Parliament's Slavery Abolition Act in 1833. His memorandum echoed the racial theories of the prominent writer Thomas

Carlyle, whose infamous *Occasional Discourse on the Negro Question*, published in both England and the United States in 1850, had blamed the demise of the West Indian sugar industry on the indolence of black people. Likewise, the "Queen's Advice" admonished the Jamaican people that their prosperity depended on "working for Wages, not uncertainly, or capriciously, but steadily and continuously, at the times when their labor is wanted, and for so long as it is wanted." Governor Eyre agreed. He had fifty thousand copies of the "Queen's Advice" printed and disseminated throughout the island.[20]

The "Queen's Advice" roiled political waters still further. Many did not believe that the queen would have written to her loyal subjects in such a fashion. Henry Clarke, an Anglican minister in the sugar parish of Westmoreland, wrote that the memorandum did not answer the people's needs and was "provoking" some to "rebellion." Clarke destroyed every copy he could find. Nevertheless, rumors spread among the peasants that the queen had sent money for their relief but that it had been stolen by colonial officials and never distributed. Other rumors claimed that the colony intended to re-enslave the peasants. And among the planters, rumors spread of a conspiracy formed among the blacks to rebel, perhaps on the first of August, the anniversary of abolition.[21]

While Taylor's memorandum was no doubt intended to give a definitive response to popular protests, it had quite the opposite effect of intensifying the tone of the Underhill meetings and spreading dissatisfaction. These developments were fostered by the activism of the Underhill Convention, a group of black political leaders who sought to make the most of this moment of political opportunity. In the parish of St. Thomas in the East, George William Gordon, a brown man who had served in the assembly before, read Underhill's letter as a call to action.[22]

Born enslaved in about 1820, Gordon was the child of an enslaved woman and Joseph Gordon, a wealthy planting attorney responsible for the management of sugar plantations for absentees in Britain. Joseph Gordon freed his son, a fairly common practice. He paid for the boy's education and set him up in business with his godfather in Black River, St. Elizabeth. The young man did well enough to establish himself as a grocer in Kingston, by which he saved enough capital to invest in land. Gordon married an Irish woman, Mary Jane Perkins, and in 1843 claimed to be worth £10,000 when he ran for the assembly for St. Thomas in the Vale, a sugar parish northwest of Spanish Town. Gordon won the seat and remained involved in politics for most of his life. He also purchased the *Jamaica Watchman and People's Free Press*, an established newspaper that had advocated for people of color since the 1820s.[23]

During his early career, Gordon's politics were not particularly radical. He voted at times with the planters—the Country Party—but he sometimes voted with the Town Party, the merchants, Jews, and politicians of color based principally in Kingston. But Gordon's politics became more radical in the early 1860s after his conversion to the Baptist faith and his embrace of the so-called Native Baptists. In 1860 and 1861, Jamaica was swept by the Great Revival, a contagious enthusiasm for the thrill of religious conversion that had begun in the United States in 1858 and spread to Jamaica in 1860. Revival was an old practice among evangelicals, and Baptist and Moravian missionaries, concerned about declining congregations on the island, fostered its spread to Jamaica. Jamaican people in hard times badly needed a spiritual lift, and the revivals swept the island. The missionaries were thrilled but also astonished by the intensity of an African revival. When a revival began, the people often took over the church, praying, singing, and dancing for eight to ten hours. And people taken with the spirit did not listen to white ministers. One missionary wrote that the revivalists "had the appearance of demoniacal possession."[24]

The Native Baptists began to emerge in the early nineteenth century as offshoots of the European missions. Missionaries had been in Jamaica since the early eighteenth century, but only the dissenting sects who arrived in the 1780s had substantial success among the slaves. In order to spread the faith, these missionaries would often allow an enslaved man to become a deacon, with the right to preach. Enslaved preachers often had much more freedom of movement than most slaves, and so they traveled and preached, and developed their own theology and practices that loosely cohered into a new Christianity. By the 1820s, European missionaries on the island began to call these independent black congregations "Native Baptists." The Native Baptist breach with orthodoxy concerned the Europeans, but they hoped that religiosity could be channeled into more "civilized" beliefs.[25]

On Christmas Day 1861, James Phillippo, the leading Baptist missionary in Kingston and author of a well-known history of Jamaica, baptized George William Gordon. After his baptism (and perhaps before) Gordon became deeply involved with the Native Baptists. He established the Tabernacle in Kingston, a chapel for the Native Baptists, and established two more chapels on his properties in St. Thomas in the East, the Rhine and the Spring. And Gordon installed the Reverend Richard Warren, an African American, as the resident pastor among the Baptists of the Blue Mountain Valley. Gordon had already been involved in the region through his investments, and he was the landlord to tenants on both properties. But after his conversion he became deeply involved with the black peasantry at the more intimate level of religion, and perhaps for the first time, began to see Jamaica through their lives.[26]

Gordon decided to reenter politics. He had left the assembly in 1849 when he declined to run for reelection to his seat. His properties occupied him and he had amassed serious debts. But after his religious conversion Gordon got involved in local politics, gaining a seat on the vestry in St. Thomas in the East, and later taking the office of magistrate. Gordon became a vocal and persistent critic of the government when the Anglican rector Stephen Cooke sent to prison a man who was poor and ill and died in confinement. In July 1862 Eyre dismissed Gordon from his office as magistrate, widely perceived as a vindictive act. And when Gordon ran for reelection to keep his seat on the vestry in July 1863, Cooke organized a movement against him.[27]

It was here that Gordon's connection with the Native Baptists became important to his political career, especially his relationship with Paul Bogle. Like Gordon, Bogle was born enslaved in about 1820, but Bogle's father had not been free and so Paul's slavery ended with abolition in 1838. Bogle was a baker and had saved enough money to buy a freehold property in the Blue Mountain Valley near the small village of Stony Gut. Bogle raised sugarcane and ground provisions such as cassava and yams; he had fruit trees and cattle, and he even experimented with the growing of cotton. Bogle and Gordon had commercial dealings as early as 1858 when Bogle shipped produce to Gordon's shop in Kingston, but with Gordon's conversion religion became a part of their bond as well. Bogle attended services at Gordon's chapel on his Spring estate, and Gordon helped Bogle raise funds to establish a chapel for the Native Baptists in Stony Gut, where Bogle would preach. And in March 1865, Gordon baptized Bogle as a deacon at the Tabernacle in Kingston.[28]

When Eyre and Cooke coordinated their efforts to remove Gordon from his political offices, Bogle had written to Gordon with a plan to regain his seat in the vestry. If Gordon could extend him a loan, Bogle could distribute it among freeholders he knew who were behind in their taxes and therefore could not vote. If these men could pay off their taxes and register as voters, they might have enough votes to gain Gordon a seat in the assembly. While we do not know if Gordon actually followed Bogle's plan, he did gain reelection to the assembly as the member from St. Thomas in the East in March 1863. He also coordinated with Bogle to elect a group of black and brown leaders to the vestry of St. Thomas in the East. Gordon became an implacable enemy of Governor Eyre, and locally he clashed with the rector Cooke and the custos of the parish, Baron von Ketelhodt. When the Underhill meetings swept the island in the spring and summer of 1865, the political divisions in St. Thomas in the East were tense and drawn.[29]

On Saturday October 7, 1865, a large crowd gathered in Morant Bay. Saturday was market day, so this was not unusual, but there was great political tension on this market day because of a case of trespass lodged against Lewis Miller of Stony Gut by Wellwood Maxwell Anderson, a brown assemblyman, agent-general of immigration, and the proprietor of Middleton Pen. Anderson's property abutted Stony Gut and was occupied largely by tenant farmers such as Miller, who refused to pay rent. Land disputes involving Anderson had been frequent since the late 1850s, and a crowd had assembled to observe the case. The presiding magistrates were both proprietors, and when they decided in favor of Anderson and slapped Miller with a heavy fine, the crowd was outraged. They called on Lewis to appeal, he did so, and his bond was posted by Paul Bogle.

But the case that started the melee involved the petty assault of one black teen against another, resulting in a fine of twelve shillings. A black spectator, James Geoghegen, urged the boy not to pay, and when the magistrate ordered Geoghegen arrested for disrupting the court, several of the crowd intervened, escorted Geoghegen outside, and beat the policemen on the courthouse steps. Two days later a contingent of black policemen were sent up to Stony Gut to arrest the men involved in the fight, including Bogle, whom the authorities assumed was behind the whole confrontation. When the police arrived in Bogle's yard and attempted to arrest him, hundreds of his supporters turned out, armed with cutlasses, clubs, and pikes. They quickly overpowered the police, beat them, and forced them to take an oath that they would "join their colour" and "cleave to the black." They sent the policemen back down to Morant Bay with the message that Bogle would come down the next day to the scheduled vestry meeting. Alarmed by Bogle's message, von Ketelhodt summoned the parish militia and wrote Governor Eyre to send troops from Kingston. The call of shells blowing could already be heard in the hills above Morant Bay.[30]

Bogle came in force. The next morning several hundred men and women came down from the hills, marching in two long columns, blowing shells and beating drums. Their numbers grew as they approached Morant Bay, and upon arrival they attacked the police station, emptying its arsenal. The parish vestry was meeting in the courthouse, and a small company of militia was gathered nearby. As the rebels approached the courthouse the militia filed out, von Ketelhodt came out on the courthouse steps, attempted to read the Riot Act, but was answered with a volley of curses and stones. The militia opened fire, killing several rebels, but before they could reload the rebels charged. The militia retreated back into the courthouse and began to fire on the crowd. The rebels set fire to the courthouse and the surrounding structures, and when these fell the terrified militia and vestrymen were lost to the crowd. Some ran and escaped, others were beaten to death; von Ketelhodt's body was found mutilated.

The rebellion spread throughout the eastern parishes and lasted several days. Governor Eyre declared martial law and dispatched troops and militia throughout the region to quell the violence. He came to Morant Bay himself on October 15 and met with a delegation of Maroons, calling upon them to meet their treaty obligations to assist the colonial state in the suppression of slave rebellions. The Maroons agreed to fight with the British.[31]

The destruction wrought by the rebels had been extensive, but the violence of the British and their allies would be worse. All told, the rebels had killed twenty-two and wounded thirty-four; they burned down five buildings in Morant Bay and plundered twenty plantations in the surrounding region. But British forces killed at least eighty-five people in their settlements in the countryside surrounding Morant Bay. They flogged more than six hundred people right there in the fields, as if they were slave rebels. They burned a thousand peasant homes, sometimes entire villages at one burst. The courts-martial they established sent 354 people to the gallows, including Paul Bogle. And in an extraordinary abuse of power,

Governor Eyre accused George William Gordon of instigating the revolt and ordered his arrest and transportation to Morant Bay, where he sat before a court-martial on the charge of treason. Gordon was hanged on October 23, 1865.[32]

The first reports of "negro insurrection" in Jamaica appeared in American newspapers within a couple days of Gordon's death. By November 3 Paul Bogle had been identified, a reward of $2,000 offered for his arrest, and the next day's papers reported that the insurgents were "besieging Kingston." The Spanish authorities in Cuba had become so concerned with the contagion of rebellion that they had sent warships to aid in the suppression. Another early report in the Lynchburg *Daily Virginian* described a "band of negroes, numbering 800 men, thoroughly organized . . . sweeping everything before them." A widely reprinted letter from William A. Isles, who worked for a brokerage firm that traded in the island, placed the revolt in a broader perspective and was highly sympathetic to the planters. Ever since emancipation, Isles wrote, "the authorities have experienced considerable opposition in attempting to collect the taxes from the negroes." Black Jamaicans were "mostly squatters," who as Carlyle had suggested were incapable of the "ordinary industry" that would have made the lands they used productive. Isles wrote that the first riot at the courthouse had stemmed from a contest over tax collection, and he described the killing of Baron von Ketelhodt with gruesome details, "thumbs" sliced off and bowels "ripped open." The rebellion "was still in progress" when he wrote, and the white population feared for their lives.[33]

News of the rebellion in Morant Bay coincided with and reinforced widespread communal fears among whites in the American South that the freedpeople would soon rise up in a rebellion of vengeance against their former masters. Known as the Christmas Insurrection Scare of 1865, the climate of fear that reigned over the South in these months reflected the visceral struggle over the terms of emancipation in the former slaveholding states. In the immediate aftermath of the war, many freedpeople began to settle on and cultivate on their own behalf the lands of their former plantations. As we have seen in Jamaica, the aspiration to own land was a common response to the abolition of slavery. In the South, wartime developments such as General Sherman's Field Order No. 15, which distributed forty acres of confiscated land to recently freed black families, encouraged the belief that a more general distribution of land might be in the works. Most black southerners had not received land from Sherman's order, but word of it spread, amplifying the urgency for land.[34]

In May 1865, President Andrew Johnson had announced the principles that would govern the reconstruction of the United States. On the condition of taking an oath of loyalty to the amended Constitution of 1864, which outlawed slavery, the president pardoned for their treason all former Confederates, with the only stipulation that high-ranking Confederate officers needed to seek a personal pardon from the president himself. With the exception of slave property, Johnson recognized all the property rights of former Confederates, which secured their property in the land they had held as slaveholders. Moreover, the president appointed provisional governors over the former Confederate states and ordered them to call state conventions empowered to amend the states' prewar constitutions. The new constitutions had to recognize the abolition of slavery, but the states could conduct the elections of delegates under prewar legislation, meaning that former slaves would not have representation in the creation of these new constitutions. The new constitutions would in turn be used by the states to apply to rejoin the United States of America.[35]

Johnson's policies allowed much of the Confederate leadership to reenter state politics. State legislatures based upon the new constitutions began to formulate the infamous Black Codes, which sought to reestablish the enslavement of black southerners in everything but name. Throughout the South, but especially in regions where plantation agriculture had prevailed, conflict developed between freedpeople who had begun to settle on former plantation lands after the war, and former plantation owners who sought to regain control of land and labor. In such a fraught political context, meetings of black laborers fostered rumors of conspiracy, which enabled whites to crack down with violence, just as they had when slavery reigned.[36]

Writers for the moderate *Springfield Republican* of Massachusetts quickly made the connection between the violence in Morant Bay and the situation in the former Confederacy. On October 27, before the *Republican* printed anything about Morant Bay, a story headlined "Crime in the South" described the recent circulation of reports that "the southern people, in one place and another, are in fear of negro insurrections and for this reason object to the removal of the United States troops." Three days later, when a newspaper from Halifax brought news of the insurrection in

Jamaica, the *Republican* printed a report and sharply observed: "The fact of their insurrection will be seized upon by the reactionists as an argument against giving the negro his freedom." But the editors argued that as no one yet knew the cause of the rebellion, "it is safe to say that it is not chargeable to the state of freedom"; rather, the violence stemmed from the "lingering barbarisms" of slavery.[37]

The next week, the *Republican* printed a story that alleged an explanation for the outbreak in Jamaica. Its reporters had learned about the petitions to the Crown for assistance, as well as the government's scornful response. The author noted the frustration this exchange induced among the people of Jamaica, but argued that the revolt had been triggered by the arrival of "a large number of brutal negroes from St. Domingo." While this seems at first like a paranoid racial fiction, there was in fact a prominent exile community of Haitians living in Kingston, and Haiti was in the midst of a civil war that had sent numerous boats with terrified migrants from Port-au-Prince to Kingston. Real-time events combined with fearful white memories of the Haitian Revolution, which had also sent refugees to Kingston. In this tumultuous moment in 1865 we can observe the distinct processes of emancipation—in Haiti, Jamaica, and the American South—become a deeply woven history of Atlantic emancipation, a history with great geographic breadth that does not follow a clean, chronological line.[38]

For the *New York World*, a sharply written Democratic paper sympathetic to the white South, the precise cause for the rebellion did not matter. What did matter was the political condition of white people in post-emancipation Jamaica. The Jamaica Assembly was "virtually and to all purposes a negro assembly, as not more than one-fifth of the members belong to the despised white race." The black population of the island outnumbered the whites "twenty to one." The mayor of Kingston was a "colored man . . . more than three-fourths of the magistrates and officers of the Colonial Government are colored men, and several of the best educated and most prominent journalists of the island are also colored men. The police . . . belong to the same race." This racial dystopia was compounded by "an infernal feeling of hatred" that black Jamaicans held against the whites. Incredibly, the *World* attributed the "principal cause" of this racial enmity to the agitation of "emissaries from the Northern United States, who go about among the . . . debased blacks, instilling false and pernicious ideas into the craniums of their too-willing hearers."

American abolitionists (or perhaps "black" Republicans) espoused the idea of a "free and independent negro republic." They would invite "the brutal Souloque"—the recently overthrown president of Haiti—to take power and "follow in the footsteps of the inhuman butchers of 1793." The *World* ended its account ominously, predicting "an indiscriminate massacre of white women and children" if the rebellion was not crushed soon.[39]

The *Daily Virginian* of Lynchburg reprinted this account in full, adding that "later reports" described "terrible massacres of the whites." The *Virginian* suggested that northern abolitionists were behind these developments and would now "transfer the scenes of Jamaica and San Domingo to the Southern States of this Union." The rebellion in Jamaica revealed to white southerners that the "spirit of old John Brown still lives though 'his body is a mouldering.'" The lessons of emancipation in the British West Indies were even more potent after the war than they had been when the white South still had slavery to defend. The focus on the political power held by Jamaican blacks foreshadowed white southerners' fear that their states would be controlled by black men. The frenzied perception of "terrible massacres" looked backward to the fear of slave rebellions and forward to the paramilitary violence of the Ku Klux Klan. Northern Democratic organs like the *World* stirred up these fears with racist portrayals of the revolt borrowed from the papers of their white Jamaican counterparts. The process of "opinion formation" in the United States about what should happen in the former slaveholding states would be shaped by such vitriolic coverage of the Morant Bay Rebellion.[40]

As these first reports of the insurrection spread throughout the United States, Jamaica underwent a radical change in its constitution. For more than two hundred years the Colonial Assembly of Jamaica had possessed both legislative authority and the power of the purse. The Crown appointed a governor, but the assembly paid his salary and so his power was limited. But stemming from developments elsewhere in the empire, especially from India after the Mutiny of 1857, the British government's Colonial Office embraced a more authoritarian mode of imperial governance that sought to strengthen the power of colonial governors by weakening local institutions such as the old assemblies. Governor Eyre embraced this view and on October 23 wrote: "There is nothing like striking whilst the iron is hot . . . if we are to get a change of constitution thro' the medium of the Assembly itself, now is the time to do it when everybody is in a state of the greatest alarm and apprehension."[41]

On November 7, in his first address to the assembly after the suppression of the rebellion, Eyre spoke gravely of the threat that Bogle, Gordon, and their people posed to Jamaica. The rebels had been "daring and determined," and Eyre claimed that their "intention has been, and still is, to make Jamaica a second Haiti." Eyre argued that members of the assembly had only "one course" of action to avert "the calamity" of having to live under a black state. He called upon the assembly to abolish the current form of colonial governance, to dissolve the institution that had long represented their interests as planters but had also nurtured a budding sovereignty among the black and brown politicians of the second generation after slavery. While there was debate and protest from the caucus of black, brown, and Jewish assemblymen, the Jamaica Assembly dissolved itself. Jamaica was thereafter ruled by a governor and a council, with six official and three unofficial members. The political space for the development of a black leadership in Jamaica had been rapidly extinguished.[42]

African American observers in the South saw the relevance of this Jamaican history as it developed. The *South Carolina Leader*, a black newspaper published in Charleston but also read aloud in the plantation regions of the state, featured regular reports on Jamaica that disputed the portrayal of events in the white newspapers. When the editors learned that some of the planters "upon the Cooper River, in the neighborhood of the Santee" feared a similar insurrection, the paper opined that such fears were utterly groundless: "A race that has remained quiet and inoffensive for upwards of two hundred years under the most oppressive system of tyranny the world has ever known, will not now, under the smiles of Liberty, attempt the destruction of the planters."[43]

The *Leader* also expressed clear statements about Reconstruction policy. In the same issue containing its dismissal of racial violence, an essay titled "The Ultimatum" stated that "Negro manhood suffrage is the obvious ultimatum of Congress to the seceded States." It was the only policy that could do justice to the black men of the South who had been loyal to the United States throughout the recent war: "The VOICE OF THE LORD GOD walking through the land summons Congress in unmistakable tones to enfranchise HIS black outcasts while it has the power to do so."[44]

The violence in Jamaica, according to this analysis, had stemmed from the same political and racial tensions that were extremely fragile in the American South. About a week after its ultimatum, the *Leader* reprinted an article from the *New York Evening Post* titled "About Negro Insurrections." The author observed that in the history of Jamaica, rebellions had been far more common under slavery than afterward. The abolition of slavery had been "the most effective of peace measures." Jamaica's recent rebellion had resulted from the "class oppression" of Jamaica's white planters against the numerically dominant blacks. The planters were well represented in the assembly, which had set property qualifications so high that less than 1 percent of the island's population had the right to vote. The rebellion had resulted from the denial of political voice, the exclusion of most of the descendants of slaves from the electorate, the denial of their right to vote.[45]

As if in direct response, the *Tri-Weekly News* of Winnsboro, South Carolina, drew precisely the opposite lessons from the rebellion in Jamaica. With vitriolic prose, the paper argued that the insurrection in Jamaica "should serve . . . as a terrible warning of what may occur here" if the "intemperate radicals" of the North were to accomplish their aims. The paper named Frederick Douglass, Wendell Phillips, Horace Greeley, and William Lloyd Garrison as the reckless agitators who wanted to give the black man the vote. The essay warned that in Jamaica it had been black voters who had elected to office George William Gordon, the man who had "inflamed the minds of his ignorant followers" and launched a bloody rebellion. This voice of the white South saw the recent history of Jamaica, alongside that of Haiti, as evidence that demonstrated "the utter incapacity of the negro race for self-government." The writer warned President Johnson "to approach this grave matter of negro equality and negro suffrage in the most careful manner."[46]

As the news of insurrections—real and imagined—helped stir the fears of southerners black and white, the Thirty-Ninth Congress convened in Washington on December 4, 1865. The Radical Republicans who controlled the Congress refused to recognize the southern delegations elected under President Johnson's criteria. Both houses therefore consisted of representatives from the northern states who had been elected before the end of the war.

Five days after the Congress convened, a delegation of 250 gentlemen of the British and Foreign Antislavery Society marched to the Colonial Office in London and presented a petition that Governor Eyre be immediately recalled from his post. British society, which had split deeply over political sympathies concerning slavery and the American Civil War, divided along the same lines on the controversy over Governor Eyre. Thomas Carlyle supported Eyre, while the philosopher John Stuart Mill and the reform leader John Bright led the demand for his removal. On December 30 the Crown established the Jamaica Royal Commission to investigate the causes of the rebellion as well as the legitimacy of the violent suppression. The investigation magnified the impact of the Morant Bay Rebellion, generating news and interest about what had happened. In the United States, these stories had immediate relevance to the status of the freedpeople of the South.[47]

With the momentous political developments of abolition and national reconstruction of such massive import during these years, American newspapers could choose a story from Jamaica and easily relate it to the American South. The *South Carolina Leader*, for example, published for its sizable audience of freedpeople an obituary of George William Gordon titled "The Jamaica Martyr." The writer compared Gordon to the Reverend John Smith, who had died in prison after being accused of instigating the slave rebellion in Demerara in 1823. And the *Leader* compared Gordon to John Brown, "who paid with his life the penalty of his noble devotion to negro freedom." The paper described Gordon as a man of about fifty who had risen from slavery to become a member of the Colonial Assembly. "His constituents [were] mostly black people," and Gordon had become "an avowed opponent of the policy which aims at the supremacy of the planter class." His enemies had murdered him because "his course of political action was calculated to open the eyes of the black people . . . to the true character of that system of legislation by which their rights have been trifled with, their interests sacrificed, and their progress retarded." We can have little doubt that African American readers of the life and death of George William Gordon understood the struggles he had faced and saw reflected in his life and death a worrisome future for themselves.[48]

The *Leader*'s editors shared their reflections on Gordon during intense discussions in the Thirty-Ninth Congress about Reconstruction policy. Radical Republicans in Congress were deeply concerned about dangerous developments in the South, and about a month before the *Leader* printed its obituary of Gordon, Senator Charles Sumner of Massachusetts demanded on the Senate floor that Carl Schurz's report on conditions in the South be read aloud. A German immigrant who had been involved in the 1848 revolutions in Europe, Schurz had emerged as an influential Republican journalist in the 1850s and had risen to the rank of major general in the Union army during the war. Under pressure from the Radicals in Congress, Johnson had sent Schurz on a tour of the South during the summer of 1865 to investigate the workings of Reconstruction policy in the South. The tension between Johnson and the Radical Republicans had deepened in the interim, and Johnson had wanted to bury Schurz's report. Sumner and Schurz were determined abolitionists and frequent correspondents. Sumner had arranged for Schurz's letters from the South to be published in the *Boston Advertiser*. On the Senate floor, Sumner pursued a public reading of the report in exchanges with two colleagues concerned that this would take too much time, but then accepted the apparent compromise of having the report printed, the latter his intention all the while. Schurz's report detailed the rise of former Confederates and the spate of violence that terrorized black communities throughout the South. It showed the Black Codes in operation, clear evidence that the president's policies had already begun to undermine the process of emancipation that had only just begun. Sumner's motion made the report available to the public as an official government report appended to a message from the president on the condition of "the States of the Union lately in rebellion." More than one hundred thousand copies were printed, and the report received extensive coverage in the Republican press in the same news cycle as the latest developments from the investigation into the rebellion in Jamaica.[49]

Sumner and Schurz shone a bright light on the horrific conditions in the South, and in early January 1866 Senator Lyman Trumbull of Illinois introduced two bills, one to extend the operations of the Freedmen's Bureau, the other to protect the civil rights of African Americans in the South. At the same time, a debate on the issue of suffrage for black men also preoccupied the Congress. Republicans realized that the Constitution had to be amended beyond the abolition of slavery, for if the southern states were to be re-admitted to the Union under the current Constitution, their delegations would still be bolstered by the three-fifths clause.

On January 31, an amendment to the Constitution proposed by the moderate Republican James Blaine of Maine passed the House. The amendment would penalize states that denied the suffrage "on account of race or color" by excluding "all persons therein of such race or color . . . from the basis of representation." The amendment created a loophole for northern states that had disenfranchised blacks and for southern states that did not wish to enfranchise former slaves. It was a compromise measure to satisfy the political desire to penalize states that had rebelled, without establishing full racial equality at the polls, which most Republicans would not accept. But on February 5, Sumner, the most radical of Republicans, launched a five-hour oration that blasted the amendment and laid out the principles of Radical Reconstruction.[50]

Sumner argued that the era of compromises over what he called "Human Rights" had ceased. It was now time to act decisively "to secure the Equal Rights of All at the ballot box." For three generations now, Americans had understood the abolition of slavery within the backdrop of the Haitian Revolution, and "only recently," Sumner reminded his audience, "we have listened to a similar tragedy from Jamaica, thus swelling the terrible testimony" of justice denied to former slaves. Drawing on abolitionist arguments that stretched back to the British abolitionist Thomas Clarkson, Sumner argued that the slave rebellion in Saint Domingue and the recent uprising in Jamaica both stemmed from "the denial of rights to colored people," first by Napoleon and more recently by the planters of Jamaica. He urged his fellow senators to imagine the unfolding of a similar history in the American South, "the unhappy freedman blasted by the ban of exclusion." If the former slave, and not the "Rebel master," were to suffer the change of slavery into freedom, "he must be discontented, restless, anxious, and smarting with . . . consciousness of rights denied." The freedmen of the South were "not unlike the freedmen of San Domingo or Jamaica," Sumner argued, "they have the same . . . sense of wrong, and the same revenge." Sumner predicted the "terrible war of races foreseen by Jefferson" if the freedmen of the South were not "enfranchised" with the full rights of American citizens, including the vote.[51]

No one drew the connections between Morant Bay, Haiti, and the American South as clearly as Sumner, but the legislation that redefined federal Reconstruction policy emphasized the protection of the political rights of black men who had once been enslaved. The Civil Rights Act, which the Congress passed over Andrew Johnson's veto on April 9, 1866, endowed with citizenship "all persons born in the United States . . . of every race and color, without regard to any previous condition of slavery or involuntary servitude." Black people would have all the rights "enjoyed by white citizens." Citizens were guaranteed the right to enforce contracts, the right to hold property, and the right to sue in court. Moreover, infractions of this law were to be tried in the federal courts, and the law would be enforced by U.S. marshals and by agents of the Freedmen's Bureau, who were instructed to "institute proceedings against any and every person who shall violate the provisions of this act." The law also established fees for officers who enforced the law, no small thing in the South's devastated economy. Congress adopted policies that many hoped would avoid the problems faced in Jamaica.[52]

The abolition of slavery spread throughout the Atlantic world in a series of historical processes that were distinct but entangled. Because of the integrated worlds of slavery created by the empires of the eighteenth century, the historical currents of these multiple emancipations flowed alongside and against each other within the broad river of historical time. Black emancipation was an Atlantic process that was slow, uneven, and interconnected.

This history begins in the U.S. North in the 1780s, becomes more radical in the Haitian Revolution; extends into the independent states of Spanish America; transforms the British Caribbean, and then the French Caribbean. An Atlantic history of emancipation then turns back to the United States, where slavery was destroyed through a brutal civil war, and then it goes to Cuba, and then Brazil. As in Haiti and the Spanish republics, it was the victors of war who established the policies that governed the process of emancipation. In political terms, the victors in the American Civil War were the Radical Republicans, members of the Thirty-Ninth Congress. It was they who would try to establish the political framework that could transform a slave society into an interracial democracy. As men who had given some thought to the problem of slavery, the members knew the stories of past emancipations through the vigorous press of their day. And if some were not readers, it would have been hard to avoid the talk about the massacre in Jamaica, the controversy over Governor Eyre, mingling with stories from the South about riots in Memphis and New Orleans.

The American press continued to draw connections between the massacre in Jamaica and the fragility of emancipation in South. During the same months that Andrew Johnson and the Radical Republicans had their epic battles over Reconstruction policy, articles in the *Atlantic Monthly*, the *New Englander*, and the *New York Times* all suggested that "the history of Jamaica plainly teaches that the slaveholder is not a safe custodian of the rights of freedmen." In an article titled "Jamaica: A Warning to the United States," the *New York Times* argued that the southern states should not be allowed to follow "the aristocratic theory of white man's government" that had proven so disastrous in Jamaica. The colonial government of Jamaica had never extended civil rights to the freedmen; there had been minimal effort at education; and the white planters had used their power to oppress the freedmen, much as they had oppressed their slaves. The *Times* warned its readers that if the old slavemasters of the South were allowed to establish states according to the same theory, "it must end in demoralizing both whites and blacks, and eventually in bloodshed far exceeding anything of the kind recorded in history."[53]

American political magazines printed these articles during the precise span of time that the nation's representatives in Congress formulated the legislation that would govern Radical Reconstruction. The Act to Provide for the More Efficient Government of the Rebel States, which passed over Johnson's veto on March 2, 1867, sought to establish the legal infrastructure necessary to implement the political mores imagined in the Civil Rights Act of the previous year. Because southern society was so violently divided by the questions of land, labor, and race, Congress ordered the rebel states to be governed directly by the U.S. Army, which would be charged with the enforcement of federal law. The act also stipulated that the former rebel states could only reapply for statehood once they had organized elections for constitutional conventions based on a voting population of male citizens, twenty-one years and older, resident in the state for at least one year, "of whatever race, color, or previous condition." All state constitutions were required to provide for universal black male suffrage, and each state would have to ratify the Fourteenth Amendment to the Constitution of the United States, which established the citizenship rights of all Americans of African descent. The law did not go so far as the freedpeople would have wanted, namely, land reform, but in a decision that seems formed by the response to the rebellion in Morant Bay, the Congress effected legislation and an enforcement mechanism to secure the political rights of black men so that they could survive the process of emancipation and establish for themselves a political future in the United States.[54]

In the making of Radical Reconstruction we can see an intersection in historical time, when the regional currents of emancipation in the Atlantic world shaped each other. The Civil Rights Act of 1866 and the First Reconstruction Act of 1867 created a coherent legislative program designed to establish civil and political rights for former slaves in a society that had long been controlled by slaveholders. These laws, as well as formative events in the South and overseas, set the stage for a radicalization of federal policy on the reconstruction of the southern states. Through the passage of these laws and the dramatic overthrow of Johnson's vetoes, the Thirty-Ninth Congress replaced a reconstruction policy that had collaborated in the maintenance of white power, with an interventionist federal policy that sought to secure the political and material rights of those freed by the war. These laws were debated, written, passed, vetoed, and passed again during the same months of intense public discussion about the meaning of the rebellion in Morant Bay. The deep similarities between the social and political transformations that both societies faced made the Morant Bay Rebellion immediately relevant to Radical Republican journalists and legislators faced with the threat of white-supremacist efforts to undermine emancipation. The Morant Bay Rebellion in Jamaica, therefore, shaped the making of Radical Reconstruction in the United States.

Notes

1. My narrative of the Morant Bay Rebellion here and later in the essay draws principally from Thomas Holt, *The Problem of Freedom: Race, Labor, and Politics in Jamaica and Britain, 1832–1938* (Baltimore: Johns Hopkins University Press, 1992), 263–309; and Gad Heuman, *"The Killing Time": The Morant Bay Rebellion in Jamaica* (London: Macmillan, 1994).

2. Jürgen Habermas, *Between Facts and Norms: Contributions to a Discourse Theory of Law and Democracy*, trans. William Rehg (Cambridge: Harvard University Press, 1996), 171, 179 (quotation), 306–7, 362–63. John Brooke's essays on Habermas are particularly helpful: "Reason and Passion in the Public Sphere: Habermas and the Cultural Historians," *Journal of Interdisciplinary History* 29 (Summer 1998): 43–67; and "Consent, Civil Society, and the Public Sphere in the Age of Revolution and the Early Republic," in *Beyond the Founders: New Approaches to the Political History of the Early American Republic*, ed. Jeffrey L. Pasley, Andrew W. Robertson, and David Waldstreicher (Chapel Hill: University of North Carolina Press, 2004), 207–50.

3. Mark Wahlgren Summers, *A Dangerous Stir: Fear, Paranoia, and the Making of Reconstruction* (Chapel Hill: University of North Carolina Press, 2009); Christopher Schmidt-Nowara, *Slavery, Freedom, and Abolition in Latin America and the Atlantic World* (Albuquerque: University of New Mexico Press, 2011); Edward Rugemer, *The Problem of Emancipation: The Caribbean Roots of the American Civil War* (Baton Rouge: Louisiana State University Press, 2008); Matthew J. Clavin, *Toussaint Louverture and the American Civil War* (Philadelphia: University of Pennsylvania Press, 2010). On historical time see Reinhart Koselleck, "Representation, Event, and Structure," in Koselleck,

Futures Past: On the Semantics of Historical Time, trans. Keith Tribe (Cambridge: MIT Press, 1985), 105–15.

4. David Beck Ryden, *West Indian Slavery and British Abolition, 1783–1807* (New York: Cambridge University Press, 2009), 40–82.

5. David Waldstreicher, *Slavery's Constitution: From Revolution to Ratification* (New York: Hill and Wang, 2009), 94–95; Matthew E. Mason, "Slavery Overshadowed: Congress Debates Prohibiting the Atlantic Slave Trade to the United States, 1806–1807," *Journal of the Early Republic* 20 (Spring 2000): 59–81.

6. David Brion Davis, *The Problem of Slavery in the Age of Revolution* (1975; reprint, New York: Oxford University Press, 1999), 446–50; Seymour Drescher, "Whose Abolition? Popular Pressure and the Ending of the British Slave Trade," *Past and Present* 143 (May 1994): 136–66; *Voyages*, http://www.slavevoyages.org/voyage/search.

7. Steven Deyle, *Carry Me Back: The Domestic Slave Trade in American Life* (New York: Oxford University Press, 2005), 15–39.

8. Seymour Drescher, *Capitalism and Antislavery: British Mobilization in Comparative Perspective* (New York: Oxford University Press, 1987), 59, 91; Manisha Sinha, *The Slave's Cause: A History of Abolition* (New Haven: Yale University Press, 2016), 130–59; James Brewer Stewart, *Holy Warriors: The Abolitionists and American Slavery*, rev. ed. (New York: Hill and Wang, 1997), 51, 66.

9. Mary Turner, *Slaves and Missionaries: The Disintegration of Jamaican Slave Society, 1787–1834* (1982; reprint, Kingston: Press University of the West Indies, 1998); Drescher, *Capitalism and Antislavery*, 106–9; Emilia Viotti da Costa, *Crowns of Glory, Tears of Blood: The Demerara Slave Rebellion of 1823* (New York: Oxford University Press, 1994); Gelien Matthews, *Caribbean Slave Revolts and the British Abolitionist Movement* (Baton Rouge: Louisiana State University Press, 2006); Edward B. Rugemer, *Slave Law and the Politics of Resistance in the Early Atlantic World* (Cambridge: Harvard University Press, 2018), chap. 7.

10. Michael Craton, *Testing the Chains: Resistance to Slavery in the British West Indies* (Ithaca: Cornell University Press, 1982), 291, 315; Turner, *Slaves and Missionaries*, 148–78. After a long period of intermittent conflict in early eighteenth century, the Jamaican Maroons signed treaties with the colonial state in 1739 that pledged them to assist the colony in the suppression of slave rebellions, among other obligations. See Rugemer, *Slave Law and the Politics of Resistance*, chap. 4.

11. Turner, *Slaves and Missionaries*, 179–91.

12. William A. Green, *British Slave Emancipation: The Sugar Colonies and the Great Experiment, 1830–1865* (New York: Oxford University Press, 1976), 119–22; Holt, *Problem of Freedom*, 42–71; Eric Foner, *Nothing but Freedom* (Baton Rouge: Louisiana State University, 1981).

13. Dale Tomich, *Through the Prism of Slavery: Labor, Capital, and World Economy* (Lanham, MD: Rowman & Littlefield, 2004), 56–71; Anthony Kaye, "The Second Slavery: Modernity in the Nineteenth-Century South and the Atlantic World," *Journal of Southern History* 75 (August 2009): 627–34. See also Rafael Marquese's contribution to this book.

14. Holt, *Problem of Freedom*, 275.

15. Bernard Semmel, *The Governor Eyre Controversy* (London: MacGibbon & Kee, 1962), 34.

16. Edward Bean Underhill, *The West Indies: Their Social and Religious Condition* (London, 1862), 441–42, 458.

17. Semmel, *Governor Eyre Controversy*, 42; E. B. Underhill, *A Letter Addressed to the Rt. Honourable E. Cardwell* (London, 1865).

18. Catherine Hall, *Civilising Subjects: Metropole and Colony in the English Imagination, 1830–1867* (Chicago: University of Chicago Press, 2002), 23–65; Semmel, *Governor Eyre Controversy*, 29–32, 39.

19. Heuman, *"Killing Time,"*44–60; Holt, *Problem of Freedom*, 269.

20. Heuman, *"Killing Time,"* 55; Rugemer, *Problem of Emancipation*, 263; Holt, *Problem of Freedom*, 42–46.

21. Heuman, *"Killing Time,"* 55–56.

22. Heuman, *"Killing Time,"* 51.

23. Heuman, *"Killing Time,"* 63; Holt, *Problem of Freedom*, 292; Swithin Wilmot, "The Road to Morant Bay: Politics in Free Jamaica, 1838–1845," *Journal of Caribbean History* 50, no. 1 (2016): 7–8.

24. Heuman, *"Killing Time,"*84.

25. Turner, *Slaves and Missionaries*, 58–59.

26. Wilmot, "The Road to Morant Bay," 9.

27. Wilmot, "The Road to Morant Bay," 9.

28. Wilmot, "The Road to Morant Bay," 11.

29. Wilmot, "The Road to Morant Bay," 9–10; Heuman, *"Killing Time,"* 66–67.

30. Holt, *Problem of Freedom*, 295–97.

31. Heuman, *"Killing Time,"* 131–32.

32. Green, *British Slave Emancipation*, 389.

33. New York *Times*, October 25, November 3, 4, 1865; Lynchburg *Daily Virginian*, November 1, 8, 1865. Isles's letter appeared first in the *Boston Traveller* and was reprinted in the *New York Times* on November 12, 1865, and in the Lynchburg *Daily Virginian* on November 16, 1865. For more on U.S. coverage of Morant Bay see Summers, *Dangerous Stir*, 57–58; Nichola Clayton, "Managing the Transition to a Free Labor Society: American Interpretations of the British West Indies during the Civil War and Reconstruction," *American Nineteenth Century History* 7, no. 1 (March 2006): 89–108; and Forest Wood, *Black Scare: The Racist Response to Emancipation and Reconstruction* (Berkeley: University of California Press, 1968), 121.

34. Dan T. Carter, "The Anatomy of Fear: The Christmas Day Insurrection Scare of 1865," *Journal of Southern History* 42, no. 3 (August 1976): 345–64; Steven Hahn, "'Extravagant Expectations' of Freedom: Rumour, Political Struggle, and the Christmas Insurrection Scare of 1865 in the American South," *Past and Present* 157 (November 1997): 129–31.

35. Eric Foner, *Reconstruction: America's Unfinished Revolution, 1863–1877* (New York: Harper and Row, 1988), 183.

36. Carter, "Anatomy of Fear," 348; Hahn, "'Extravagant Expectations,'" 126.

37. *Springfield Republican*, October 27 and 30, 1865.

38. *Springfield Republican*, November 6, 1865. On the relationship between Haiti and Jamaica during these years see Matthew J. Smith, *Liberty, Fraternity, Exile: Haiti and Jamaica after Emancipation* (Chapel Hill: University of North Carolina Press, 2014), 136–63.

39. *New York World* quoted in Lynchburg *Daily Virginian*, November 11, 1865.

40. Lynchburg *Daily Virginian*, November 11, 1865.

41. Quoted in Heuman, "*Killing Time*," 159. On imperial dimensions see John M. Mackenzie, "Empire and Metropolitan Cultures," in *The Oxford History of the British Empire*, ed. Andrew Porter, 4 vols. (New York: Oxford University Press, 1999), 3:280–81.

42. Quoted in Smith, *Liberty, Fraternity, Exile*, 160; Gad Heuman, *Between Black and White: Race, Politics, and the Free Coloreds in Jamaica, 1792–1865* (Westport, CN: Greenwood Press, 1981), 192–93.

43. "Affairs about Home," *South Carolina Leader*, December 9, 1865.

44. "Affairs about Home" and "The Ultimatum," *South Carolina Leader*, December 9, 1865.

45. "About Negro Insurrections," *South Carolina Leader*, December 16, 1865.

46. *Tri-Weekly News* (Winnsboro, SC), December 9, 1865.

47. Foner, *Reconstruction*, 228; Semmel, *Governor Eyre Controversy*, 23.

48. "The Jamaica Martyr," *South Carolina Leader*, January 27, 1866.

49. Cong. Globe, 39th Cong., 1st Sess. 79 (1865); Carl Schurz, *Report on the Condition of the South* (1866; reprint, New York: Arno, 1969); Hans L. Trefousse, *Carl Schurz: A Biography* (Knoxville: University of Tennessee Press, 1982), 154–60.

50. Foner, *Reconstruction*, 252–53; David Donald, *Charles Sumner and the Rights of Man* (New York: Knopf, 1970), 245–47.

51. Charles Sumner, "The Equal Rights of All: The Great Guaranty and Present Necessity, for the Sake of Security, and to Maintain a Republican Government," in *Charles Sumner: His Complete Works*, 20 vols. (Boston: Lee and Shepard, 1874), 13:124, 131–33. Sumner's speech was reprinted in the *New York Times*, February 6, 1866, among other newspapers, and as a pamphlet.

52. An Act to Protect All Persons in the United States in Their Civil Rights, April 9, 1866, 15 Stat., 39th Cong., 1st Sess., ch. 31, p. 27.

53. G. Reynolds, "The Late Insurrection in Jamaica," *Atlantic Monthly*, April 1866, 480–89; "The Late Insurrection in Jamaica," *New Englander* 26, no. 1 (January 1867): 53–69; "Jamaica: A Warning to the United States," *New York Times*, September 1, 1867.

54. An Act to Provide for the More Efficient Government of the Rebel States, March 23, 1867, 15 Stat., 39th Cong., 2nd Sess., ch. 153, pp. 428–30.

Contributors

Don H. Doyle is the author or editor of several books on the United States, the American South, and international history. His most recent book is *The Cause of All Nations: An International History of the American Civil War*. He is currently working on a sequel dealing with the years of Reconstruction. He has taught at several universities in the United States, Italy, England, Brazil, and France and recently retired as McCausland Professor of History Emeritus, University of South Carolina.

William A. Link is Richard J. Milbauer Professor of History at the University of Florida. He is a historian of the South whose works include *Atlanta, Cradle of the New South: Race and Remembering in the Civil War's Aftermath* and *Southern Crucible: The Making of An American Region*.

Rafael Marquese is professor of history at the University of São Paulo. Among other books, he is coauthor, with Tâmis Parron and Márcia Berbel, of *Slavery and Politics: Brazil and Cuba, 1790–1850*.

Edward B. Rugemer is associate professor of history and African American studies at Yale University. He is the author of *The Problem of Emancipation: The Caribbean Roots of the American Civil War* and *Slave Law and the Politics of Resistance in the Early Atlantic World*.

Index

Page numbers in *italics* refer to illustrations.

Abolition and emancipation: Atlantic world and, 3, 7–8, 9, 83, 84, 99, 106, 107; Baptists and, 90; Brazil and, 5, 12, 15–16, 17–18, 22, 25–27, 30, 36, 37–38, 39; Caribbean and, 14, 84, 88–89; Great Britain and, 7, 8, 18, 53, 84, 85, 86–87, 88–89, 91, 105; Haitian Revolution and, 105; Jamaica and, 7, 8, 81, 82, 83, 89, 90, 94, 97, 99–100, 102; scholarship on, 29, 86
Abolition and emancipation (United States): Confederate general on, 89; former Confederate states and, 98; impact of, on Brazil, 5, 13–14, 25–27, 39; international influences on, 8–9, 14, 82, 83–84, 86, 97–100, 103, 106–8; Presidential Reconstruction and, 103–4; Radical Republicans and, 82, 104–5; scholarship on, 2, 3, 9, 14, 15–16, 17–18, 29, 41n11, 47; supporters of, 18, 59, 82, 86
"About Negro Insurrections," 102
Act for the Abolition of the Slave Trade (Great Britain), 85
Act of Abolition (Great Britain), 84
Act to Provide for the More Efficient Government of the Rebel States (U.S.), 107
Adams, Charles Francis, 53
Africa, 89
African Americans. *See* Blacks
Alabama, 86
Alabama (ship), 47
Alaska, 6, 49, 50, 56
Allen, William H., 65
American Legion of Honor, 7
Anderson, Wellwood Maxwell, 95
Anglicans, 92, 94
Appomattox, VA, 54
Araras, Brazil, 13
Argentina, 21, 37, 38
Asians, 26, 89
Atlantic Monthly, 106
Atlantic world. *See under* Abolition and emancipation; Slavery
Australia, 37, 91
Austria, 71, 79n73

Báez, Buenaventura, 57
Baker, Bruce E., 40n7
Baptist Missionary Society, 90
Baptists, 81, 87, 90, 93–94
Barbados, 87
Baton Rouge, LA, 69
Bazaine, François Achille, 67, 70
Beckford, William, 84
Belgium, 79n73
Between Facts and Norms (Habermas), 82
Bigelow, John, 53, 67, 68, 69
Black Codes (U.S.), 2, 27, 98, 104
Black Reconstruction (Du Bois), 1, 14

Black River, St. Elizabeth, Jamaica, 92
Blacks: Jamaican, 8, 81, 89–90, 91, 93, 94, 95, 97, 100, 101, 102; U.S., 1, 2, 3, 27–28, 35, 65, 82, 97–98, 101, 104, 105–6, 107–8
Blaine, James, 104
Bleby, Henry, 88
Blight, David, 41n13
Blue Mountain Valley, 94
Bogle, Paul, 81, 94–95, 96, 97, 101
Bolivia, 56
Booth, John Wilkes, 61
Boston Advertiser, 104
Boston Traveller, 110n33
Braudel, Fernand, 42n17
Brazil: Center South of, 21, 22, 25, 29; and economy, 4, 5, 15; and Great Britain, 21; and immigrant labor, 5, 26, 35, 36–37, 38; and Jamaica, 89; and Louisiana Purchase Exposition, 11, 12–13, 29–30; and Paraguayan War, 21; political leaders in, 13, 37–38, 39; press in, 21; and railroads, 24, 26; scholarship on, 15, 16; and slave trade, 20, 21, 22, 24–25, 39; and sugar industry, 89; and United States, 18, 19, 20. *See also* Abolition and emancipation: Brazil and; Coffee production; Slavery, Brazilian
Bright, John, 103
British and Foreign Antislavery Society, 102
British West Indies, 27
Broomall, James, 41n13
Brown, John, 103
Brown, Thomas J., 41n13
Brownsville, TX, 64
Burchell, Thomas, 87–88

Café para a estação (Ferrigno), *36*
California, 61
Canada, 6, 51, 56, 74n6
Cardwell, Edward, 90–91
Caribbean: and abolition and emancipation, 14, 84, 88–89; coffee production in, 20; and European powers, 49, 51, 58, 106; scholarship on, 14; and slavery, 17, 106; and United States, 48, 49
Carlota/Charlotte of Mexico, 70
Carlyle, Thomas, 91–92, 97, 103
Catholic Church, 72
Centennial International Exhibition, 11
Central America, 48
Ceylon, 23
Charleston, SC, 101
Chicago, IL, 37
Chihuahua, Mexico, 54, 65, 66
Chile, 50, 53–54, 56
Christmas Insurrection Scare of 1865, 97
Civil Rights Act of 1866 (U.S.), 9, 82, 105–6, 107
Civil War: Caribbean and, 49; Cuba and, 50–51; European powers and, 6–7, 49, 50–51, 56, 61; federal power after, 11; Great Britain and, 102; impact of, in United States, 82–83; impact of, on Brazilian slavery, 26; industrial capitalism after, 11; Jamaica and, 83; Latin America and, 53–54; Mexico and, 59, 60–61; and Monroe Doctrine, 57; peace talks during, 57; Peninsular Campaign of, 52; Radical Republicans and, 106; republicanism after, 21; scholarship on, 1, 2, 3, 16, 47; and slavery, 17, 26, 106
Clarke, Henry, 92
Clarkson, Thomas, 105
Coffee: demand for, 17, 37; locations where produced, 12, 23, 26; marketing of, 23; prices for, 12, 18–19, 23, 26, 34, 39; tariffs on, 18–19; United States and, 5, 12, 18, 20, 22–23, 26, 37; uses of, 20; varieties of, 12
Coffee production: and age, 31, 32; Ferrigno paintings of, 13, 14, 29–30, 31, 32, *33–34*, 35; and gender, 31–32; locations of, 21, 24, 35, 37, 39; mechanization of, 13; new shrubs and, 25; organization of, 19–20, 25–26, 31–35; and race, 13, 32, 35; and slavery, 5, 20, 22, 24–25, 26, 30–31, 34, 35; steps in, 13, 30, 31–34;

and transportation, 24; volume of, 20, 22–24, 38, 39; and wages, 38; and worker housing, 29, 30, 31
Cold War, 74n10
Colheita (Ferrigno), *31*
Colombia, 23
Colonato system, 29, 30, 31–35, 36, 38
Colonial Assembly. *See* Jamaica Assembly
Colonial Office, 100, 102
Confederates: and Mexico, 7, 60–61, 62, 65–66, 67, 70; pardoning of, 98; as post-war leaders, 83, 98, 104; and property rights, 98
Confederate States of America: and European powers, 50–51, 56, 57, 61; and Mexico, 7, 57, 60; and naval war, 49, 51, 60, 90; and re-admission to United States, 2, 81, 98, 104, 107; representatives of, 51, 61; surrender of, 4; William Seward and, 7, 56, 57
Congress, U.S.: and 13th Amendment, 49; abolitionists and, 86; and Andrew Johnson, 49, 68, 102, 104, 105, 106, 107, 108; and emancipation, 82; former Confederates in, 102; and Monroe Doctrine, 6, 58; and press, 82, 101, 103, 107; and Reconstruction, 2, 6, 8, 9, 10, 82, 83, 103–6, 107–8; and transatlantic slave trade, 84; and U.S. territorial expansion, 49–50
Constitution, U.S.: 13th Amendment to, 49; 14th Amendment to, 2, 9, 104–5, 107; 15th Amendment to, 2, 9; former Confederates and, 98; and protection of slavery, 4; slavery compromise in, 84–85
Cooke, Stephen, 94, 95
Cooper River, 101
Cooper Union, 59
Corps Législatif, 53, 69
Costa Rica, 23
Cotton, 4, 5, 15, 17, 18, 19–20
Country Party, 93
Cuba: and Jamaica, 85, 89; and Lincoln's assassination, 54; and Morant Bay Rebellion, 97; and slavery, 16, 17, 54, 106; and Spain, 56; and sugar industry, 89; and transatlantic slave trade, 85; and United States, 49, 50–51, 54
Cuidad Juárez, Mexico, 66

Daily Virginian, 97, 100, 110n33
Danish Virgin Islands, 49
Davis, Jefferson, 60–61
Defenders of the Monroe Doctrine, 64
Demerara, 87, 103
Democratic peace theory, 74n10
Democratic Republicans, 85
Denmark, 50, 83
Díaz, Porfirio, 72
Dominican Republic, 7, 50, 57, 58
Dom Pedro II (emperor of Brazil), 21, 22
Douglass, Frederick, 102
Doyle, Dan, 4, 6, 7, 9
Du Bois, W.E.B., 1, 2, 14, 40n7
Duniway, Clyde Augustus, 79n80
Dunning, William A., 2
Dunning School, 41n13
Dutch East Indies, 12

Ecuador, 56
Edwards, Bryan, 84
El Salvador, 23
Emancipation. *See* Abolition and emancipation
Empire of Brazil. *See* Brazil
Ensacamento do café (Ferrigno), *34*
Eugénie de Montijo (empress), 70
Europe: 1848 revolutions in, 103; and Caribbean, 49, 58; and execution of Maximilian I, 70–71, 72; grain prices in, 37; labor from, 36; and Latin America, 50; liberals in, 52, 53, 55–56, 57; and Lincoln's assassination, 52–53; and Mexico, 6; and Monroe Doctrine, 50, 58; railroads in, 24; and religion, 59; and South America, 58; and United States, 20, 49, 50, 57, 61; and Western

Europe—*continued*
Hemisphere, 55–56; William Seward and, 6, 49. *See also* France; Germany; Great Britain; Italy
Exhibitions, 11, 12, 14, 39n2
Eyre, Edward: career of, 91; controversy over, 102–3, 106; and George William Gordon, 91, 94, 95, 97; and Jamaican constitution, 100–101; and Jamaican people, 92; and Morant Bay Rebellion, 81, 96, 97; and Underhill letter, 91

Ferrigno, Antonio, 13. *See also* Coffee production: Ferrigno paintings of
First Reconstruction Act of 1867 (U.S.), 82, 107
Fish, Hamilton, 49
Florada (Ferrigno), *30*
Foner, Eric, 14–15, 40n8, 41n13, 73n1
Foreign Slave Trade Act (Great Britain), 85
Fort Sumter, 51
France: and Great Britain, 85; and Latin America, 51, 54; liberals in, 64, 69; and Lincoln's assassination, 53, 69; and Mexico, 6–7, 49, 51, 55, 56, 57, 58, 59, 62, 63, 64, 66–67, 68–71, 79n80; and Monroe Doctrine, 52; and religion, 51, 59; Second Empire in, 53; and slavery, 83, 106; and United States, 51, 53, 57, 60, 61, 62, 63, 64, 67–69, 79n73, 79n80
Freedmen's Bureau, 104, 105–6
Free Womb Law (Brazil), 21, 22, 25, 26
Friends of Mexico clubs, 59, 64
Fuller, Stephen, 84

Garibaldi, Giuseppe, 71
Garrison, William Lloyd, 102
Geoghegen, James, 95
Georgia, 84, 85
Germany, 47
"Get Out of Mexico!," 64
Gispen, Kees, 15
Gordon, George William, 91, 92–95, 97, 101, 102, 103
Gordon, Joseph, 92
Grant, Ulysses S.: and Mexico, 60, 61–63, 64, 65, 66, 67, 69, 72; military service of, 60
Great Britain: and abolition and emancipation, 7, 8, 18, 53, 84, 85, 86–87, 88–89, 91, 105, 106; and Brazil, 21; and Canada, 6, 51, 56; and Caribbean, 51; and colonial government, 100; and economy, 17; and France, 85; and Irish American Fenians, 56; and Lincoln's assassination, 53; and Mexico, 6; and Monroe Doctrine, 52; and Morant Bay Rebellion, 81, 103; and North America, 6, 48, 56; publication of Carlyle's *Occasional Discourse on the Negro Question* in, 92; and Russia, 56; and slavery, 18, 20, 83, 86, 106; and transatlantic slave trade, 84, 85, 86–87; and United States, 19, 51, 56, 57, 102
Greeley, Horace, 102
Green, George Mason, 65
Guatemala, 23
Gwin, William, 61

Habermas, Jürgen, 8, 82
Hahn, Steven, 15–16, 39, 41n13
Haiti: emancipation in, 99, 101, 102, 105, 106; emergence of, 83; uprisings in, 99, 100, 101. *See also* Saint Domingue/San Domingo
Haitian Revolution, 85, 99, 105, 106
Haitians, 99
Halifax, Nova Scotia, 98
Hampton Roads, VA, 57
Haussmann, Georges-Eugène, 71
Havana, Cuba, 50–51, 54
HMS *Trent*, 51
Hobsbawm, Eric, 39n2
Homestead Act (U.S.), 37
Honduras, 23
Hugo, Victor, 71

Illinois, 104
India, 100
Isles, William A., 97, 110n33
Italy and Italians, 5, 36–37, 38, 47

Jamaica: 1831 slave uprising in, 87–88; Anglicans in, 92, 94; Baptists in, 87; and Brazil, 89; constitution of, 100–101; crime in, 90, 95; Crown lands in, 91; and Cuba, 85, 89; and education, 90; and emancipation, 7–8, 83, 89–90, 94; franchise in, 89–90, 102; Great Revival in, 93; and immigration, 89; importance of, 84; inequality in, 7–8; Jews in, 90, 93, 101; Methodists in, 87; missionaries in, 87, 88, 90, 93; Morant Bay Rebellion in, 7–9, 81–82, 95–97, 102; Moravians in, 93; newspapers in, 91, 93; parishes in, 91, 92, 94, 95; political parties in, 93; poverty in, 90; prices in, 90; sugar industry in, 84, 89; tax code in, 89; and transatlantic slave trade, 89; and Underhill meetings, 91–92, 95; unemployment in, 90; and U.S. Civil War, 83, 90; wages in, 89, 90
Jamaica Assembly, 89, 99, 100, 101
"Jamaica: A Warning to the United States," 106–7
"Jamaica Martyr, The," 103
Jamaicans: blacks, 81, 89–90, 91, 93, 94, 95, 97, 100, 101, 102; browns, 90, 91, 92, 95, 101; Maroons, 87, 96, 109n10
Jamaica Royal Commission, 103
Jamaica Watchman and People's Free Press, 93
James, C.L.R., 14
Japan, 47
Java, 23
Jefferson, Thomas, 85
Jerome Napoleon, 68
Jews, 90, 93, 101
Jiménez, Michael F., 23
Johnson, Andrew: and civil rights, 59; and diplomacy, 56; and former Confederates, 98, 102; and impeachment crisis, 56; and Mexico, 59–60, 61, 63, 68; and Radical Republicans, 49, 104, 106; and Reconstruction, 2, 59, 98, 104; vetoes by, 105, 107, 108; and William Seward, 48, 49, 56
Juárez, Benito: and Confederate surrender, 54; death of, 72; and execution of Maximilian I, 70, 71; and Lincoln's assassination, 54; Napoleon III on, 69; political rivals of, 65; and United States, 71, 97; and war against Second Mexican Empire, 48, 56, 62, 65, 66–67, 69
Jurien de La Gravière, Edmond, 68

Kelly, Brian, 40n7
Kerr-Ritchie, Jeffrey R., 16, 41n11
Kingston, Jamaica, 92, 93, 94, 97, 99
Kirby Smith, Edmund, 62
Kolchin, Peter, 3
Koselleck, Reinhart, 42n17
Ku Klux Klan, 100

LaFeber, Walter, 47, 48
Lally, Frank Edward, 79n80
Latin America: and European powers, 50, 51, 54; liberals in, 57, 58; and Lincoln's assassination, 53; and Monroe Doctrine, 6, 49, 54, 58, 60; and slavery, 5; and United States, 49, 56
Lavadouro (Ferrigno), *33*
Leavitt, Joshua, 59
Lima, Peru, 58
Lincoln, Abraham: assassination of, 51, 52–53, 54–55, 61, 69, 91; and Civil War, 53–54; and diplomacy, 56; election of, 37; and Mexico, 59; reelection of, 51; and William Seward, 48
Lincoln, Mary Todd, 53
Link, William A., 41n13
Long Depression, 23
Louisiana, 20, 86

Louisiana Purchase Exposition, 11–12, 13, 32, 38, 39
Louis Napoleon. *See* Napoleon III
Lynchburg, VA, 97, 100, 110n33

Manet, Édouard, 71
Marquese, Rafael, 4–5, 6, 9
Martí, José, 54
Maryland, 86
Massachusetts, 98, 103
Matamoros, Mexico, 60, 63, 66
Maury, Matthew Fontaine, 61
Maximilian I: assumption of throne by, 7, 58; and Black Decree, 67, 71; and Confederates, 60–61, 67; European opposition to, 57; execution of, 7, 70–71, *72*; and France, 7, 56, 57, 58, 61, 67, 69, 70; goals of, 70; Mexican opposition to, 7, 56, 58, 60, 69, 70; scholarship on, 70; and slavery, 61, 67; and United States, 7, 60–61, 62, 63, 64–65, 66, 67, 79n73
Mazzini, Giuseppe, 57
McClellan, George, 52
Mejía, Tomás, *72*
Memphis, TN, 106
Methodists, 87
Mexican Emigration Company, 65
Mexico: and Confederates, 7, 60–61, 62; European invasion of, 6–7; and European powers, 53–54; and France, 6–7, 49, 51, 55, 56, 57, 58, 59, 62, 63, 64, 66–67, 68–72, 79n80; and Lincoln's assassination, 54–55; as part of North America, 74n6; and religion, 51, 59, 72; and slavery, 61; and Spain, 52; Ulysses S. Grant and, 60, 61–64; and United States, 48, 49, 55, 59, 60, 61–69, 72, 78n55, 78n58, 79n73
Mexico City, Mexico, 70
Midwest, U.S., 23, 36
Mill, John Stuart, 103
Miller, Lewis, 95
Minas Gerais, Brazil, 22, 25
Miramón, Miguel, *72*
Mississippi, 28, 86
Moniteur, 71
Monroe, James, 6
Monroe Doctrine: during Civil War, 57; European powers and, 50, 52; Latin America and, 6, 49, 54; popular support for, 64; post-Civil War use of, 57–59, 60; premise of, 6, 49, 57; William Seward and, 6, 49
Monroe League, 64
Monroe Palace, 11
Montego Bay, Jamaica, 87, 88
Monterrey, Mexico, 66
Morant Bay Rebellion: causes of, 7–8, 9; Cuba and, 97; details of, 81, 95–97; Great Britain and, 8, 81, 103; Radical Republicans and, 105, 106; United States and, 81–82, 108; U.S. press and, 9, 97, 98–100, 101, 102, 106–7, 110n33
Moravians, 93
Mutiny of 1857, 100

Napoleon I, 105
Napoleon III: and ban on political meetings and speech, 53; and canals, 51; and execution of Maximilian I, 71; and Mexico, 51, 60, 61, 64, 67, 68–70; Republicans and, 60; resistance to, 51; and United States, 65, 67–69
Nashville, TN, 60
Native Baptists, 81, 93, 94. *See also* Baptists
Nelson, Thomas, 54
Netherlands, 83
New England, 23, 84
New Englander, 106
New Orleans, LA, 64, 106
Newspapers. *See* Press
New York, NY, 12, 18–19, 59
New York Evening Post, 102
New York State, 84
New York Times, 65, 106–7, 110n33
New York Union, 65
New York World, 99–100

New Zealand, 91
North, U.S., 83, 104, 106
Nothing but Freedom (Foner), 3
Nullification Crisis, 18

Occasional Discourse on the Negro Question (Carlyle), 92
"Oh! I Vants to Go Home," 64
Ortega, Gonzales, 65
O terreiro (Ferrigno), *33*

Pacific Ocean, 49
Paraguay, 21
Paraguayan War, 21
Paraíba Valley, Brazil, 24, 37
Paris, France, 67–68, 69, 71
Parliament (Great Britain): and abolition, 85, 86–87, 88, 91; and Brazil, 21; and free trade, 89; and transatlantic slave trade, 84, 85
Paso del Norte, Mexico, 66
Paulista Party (Brazil), 38
Peace Democrats, 51
Pelletan, Eugène, 53
Pennsylvania, 84
Perkins, Mary Jane, 92
Peru, 50, 53–54, 56, 58
Philadelphia, PA, 11
Philippines, 12
Phillippo, James, 93
Phillips, Wendell, 102
Pius IX (pope), 70
Port-au-Prince, Haiti, 99
Portuguese, 38
Prado, Antônio, 36
Prado, Martinho, Jr., 36
Prates, Eduardo, 13
Press: and 1819 Jamaica uprising, 88; black, 101; British, 88; Jamaican, 91, 93; and Louisiana Purchase Exposition, 13; and Morant Bay Rebellion, 9, 97, 101, 102, 103, 106–7, 110n33; and Reconstruction, 8; Republican, 104; scholarship on, 82; and Schurz report on South, 104; on southern racial relations, 98; U.S., 9, 97, 98–100, 101, 103, 104, 106–7
Prim, Juan, 52, 57

"Queen's Advice" (Taylor), 92
Querétaro, Mexico, 70, 71

Radical Republicans: and Andrew Johnson, 49, 104, 106; and Black Codes, 27; and black rights, 105; and Civil War, 106; and emancipation, 82; and freedpersons, 82; influences on, 82–83; and Mexico, 59; and Morant Bay Rebellion, 9, 105, 108; and Reconstruction, 8, 103; and southern congressional delegations, 102. *See also* Republicans
Railroads, 24, 26
Reconstruction: and agrarian reform, 27; dates of, 4–5; and emancipation, 1, 82; and historiography of abolition, 83; influences on, 83–84; international implications of, 3; legislation during, 2, 27, 82; Midwest during, 37; Presidential, 27, 82, 98, 104, 108; Radical, 28, 38, 72, 82, 84, 105–6, 107; scholarship on, 1, 2–3, 6, 14–16, 40n8, 41n13, 47, 73n1; and sharecropping system, 14
Reconstruction (Foner), 3
Reconstructions: New Perspectives on the Postbellum United States (Brown), 41n13
Reform Bill of 1832 (Great Britain), 88
Republicans, 28, 37, 51, 58, 104, 105. *See also* Radical Republicans
Rethinking American Emancipation (Link and Broomall), 41n13
Richardson, Robert, 89
Rio de Janeiro, Brazil, 11, 12, 19, 22, 25, 26–27
Rio de Janeiro Agricultural Congress, 26–27, 36
Rio Grande, 60, 62, 66, 69
Riot Act (Jamaica), 96

River Plate zone, 21
Romero, Matías, 59, 60, 62, 63, 64, 71, 72
Rugemer, Edward, 4, 7, 8, 9, 40n8
Russia, 6, 48, 56

Saint Domingue/San Domingo: emancipation in, 83; and European powers, 53–54, 56; and migration, 99; territory available in, 49; uprisings in, 99, 100, 105; and U.S. Civil War, 56. *See also* Haiti
Saint Louis, MO, 11
San Antonio, TX, 66
San Francisco, CA, 64, 65
San Louis Potosí/San Luis de Potosí, Mexico, 66, 69
Santa Gertrudes coffee plantation (Araras, Brazil): and drying of coffee cherries, 32–34; extent of, 32; immigrants and, 38; organization of, 30–31, 32; owner of, 13; paintings depicting, 13, 14, 29–30, 31, 32, *33–34*, 35, *36;* reputation of, 13; and workers' housing, 30–31
Santee River, 101
Santiago, Chile, 54
Santos, Brazil, 12, 38
São Paulo, Brazil: and coffee production, 22, 24, 29, 35, 37–38, 39; and immigration, 38, 39; and Louisiana Purchase Exposition, 12; political leaders from, 13; and railroads, 24; and slavery and slave trade, 25
Saraiva-Cotegip Law (Brazil), 25
Schofield, John M., 62, 67–69
Schurz, Carl, 103–4
Second Slavery theory, 5, 16–17, 42n17. *See also* Slavery, Brazilian: and Second Slavery; Slavery, U.S.: and Second Slavery
Serra do Mar, 24
Seward, William: and Alaska, 6, 49, 50, 56; and Andrew Johnson, 48, 49, 56; death of, 72; and European powers, 6, 48–49; injuries to, 61; and Maximilian I, 71; and Mexico, 56, 61, 63–64, 66, 67, 68, 69, 72, 79n73; positions of, 74n10; and race, 7, 49; and Reconstruction, 49; and republican ideals, 57; scholarship on, 48, 76n39; as secretary of state, 48–49, 52, 56–57; and slavery, 49; and Thirteenth Amendment, 49; and U.S. Civil War, 49, 53–54, 56–57, 59; and U.S. expansion, 48, 49–50, 56–57
Sharpe, Samuel, 87
Shelby, Jo, 61, 66
Sheridan, Phil, 62, 65, 66, 67, 69, 72
Sherman, William Tecumseh, 97–98
Slave Registration Act (Great Britain), 86
Slavery: Atlantic world and, 5, 17–18, 83; Caribbean and, 14, 17, 20, 27, 86–87, 89, 106; Cuba and, 54, 106; Denmark and, 83; France and, 83, 106; Great Britain and, 18, 20, 83, 86, 88, 106; Jamaican, 109n10; Netherlands and, 83; Spanish and, 50
Slavery, Brazilian: and coffee, 5, 18, 19, 20, 21, 22, 24–25, 30; defense of, 18; expansion of, 5, 17, 20–21; and global economy, 5; scholarship on, 5, 15, 16–18; and Second Slavery, 5, 16, 17–18, 19, 21, 37, 39, 89; and slave trade, 20, 21, 22, 24–25; and sugar industry, 89; and U.S. emancipation and Reconstruction, 26, 39; and violence, 25. *See also* Abolition and emancipation: Brazil and
Slavery, U.S.: conditions of, 27, 29; and Constitutional compromise, 84–85; and corn, 19–20; and cotton, 5, 18, 19–20, 26, 27; defense of, 18; expansion of, 17, 20–21; and global economy, 5; scholarship on, 1, 3, 4, 15, 16–18; and Second Slavery, 5, 16, 17–18, 19, 39. *See also* Abolition and emancipation (United States)
Slavery Abolition Act (Great Britain), 88–89, 91
Slaves: and abolitionists, 25; Jamaican, 93; and missionaries, 87, 93; natural

reproduction of, 20–21; and religion, 93; and resistance, 25, 86–87, 109n10
Slave trade: internal, 20, 22, 24–25, 84, 86; transatlantic, 20, 21, 39, 84–85
Smith, John, 103
Smith, Mark M., 73n1
Sociedade Promotora de Imigração (SPI), 38
Sonora, Mexico, 61, 64
Souloque, Faustin, 100
South, U.S.: Black Codes in, 2, 27, 98, 104; and economy, 15, 19–20, 27, 28–29, 85; and emancipation, 83; freedpersons in, 27–28, 97–98; and immigration, 35–36; investigative tour of, 104; and Morant Bay Rebellion, 97; planters in, 15–16, 27, 28, 98; press on, 107; and racial violence, 83, 100, 101, 104, 106; and Radical Reconstruction, 27, 28, 107; Republican Party in, 28; scholarship on, 15–16, 39; and slavery, 4, 17, 27, 85; wages in, 36
South America, 48, 58, 74n6
South Carolina, 84–85
South Carolina Leader, 101–2, 103
Spain: and Latin America, 6, 7, 50, 52, 54, 56, 58; and Monroe Doctrine, 52; and slavery, 50; and United States, 47, 50–51, 57
Spaniards, 38
Spanish-American War, 12, 47
Spanish Town, Jamaica, 81, 92
Springfield Republican, 98–99
Stony Gut, Jamaica, 81, 94, 95
St. Thomas, 50
St. Vincent's, 91
Suez Canal, 51
Summers, Mark, 82
Sumner, Charles, 9, 103, 104, 105

Tabasco, Mexico, 54
Tabernacle, 93, 94
Taylor, Henry, 91–92
Texas, 62
Third Pan-American Conference, 11
Tomich, Dale, 5, 16–17
Town Party, 93
Tri-Weekly News, 102
Trumbull, Lyman, 104

Ukraine, 37
Underhill, Edward, 90, 91
Underhill Convention, 92
United States: and Brazil, 18, 19, 20, 26–27; and Caribbean, 48, 49; and Central America, 48; and coffee, 5, 12, 18, 20, 22–23, 26; and commercial expansion, 49, 50; and economy, 4, 5, 14, 15, 23, 28–29, 37, 48; and Europe, 20; European liberals and, 55–56; and France, 55, 60, 61, 62, 63, 64, 67–69, 79n73, 79n80; and Great Britain, 19, 56; Great Revival in, 93; and immigration, 35, 38; and imperialism, 47–48; and Jamaica, 83–84; and Mexico, 48, 55, 59–60, 61–69, 72, 78n55, 78n58, 79n73; as military power, 2; military strength of, 51–52; and Morant Bay Rebellion, 81–82, 84; and Pacific, 49; population growth in, 23; publication of Carlyle's *Occasional Discourse on the Negro* in, 92; and race, 50, 72; railroads in, 24; scholarship on, 15, 16, 47–48; and slavery, 16, 20–21, 25, 27; and slave trade, 20, 84–85, 86; and South America, 48; and Spain, 47; and tariffs, 18, 23; and territorial expansion, 23, 48, 49–50, 56; wages in, 36
United States Colored Troops, 65
Universal Exposition, 71
Uruguay, 21
U.S. Army, 7, 107
U.S. Department of State, 49

Vale do Paraíba, Brazil, 24, 37
Valparaíso, Chile, 54
Veneto region, Italy, 36, 37
Venezuela, 23
Virginia, 84, 86

Virgin Islands, Danish, 49
Viscount of Rio Branco, 22
Von Ketelhodt, Maximilian August, 95, 96, 97

War of Reform, 71
Warren, Richard, 94
Welles, Gideon, 64
"We'll Go with Grant Again," 64–65
West Africa, 85
West Indies, The: Their Social and Religious Condition (Underhill), 90
What Made the South Different? (Gispen), 15
Wilberforce, William, 88
Williams, Eric, 14
Williams, William Appleman, 47–48
Winnsboro, SC, 102
Woodward, C. Vann, 40n8
World the Civil War Made, The (Downs and Masur), 16

"Yankee Doodle Dandy," 68
Yeaman, George, 50
Yemen, 12
Yorkshire, Eng., 91

FRONTIERS OF THE AMERICAN SOUTH

Edited by William A. Link

United States Reconstruction across the Americas, edited by William A. Link (2019)

CPSIA information can be obtained
at www.ICGtesting.com
Printed in the USA
LVHW091046100519
617334LV00002B/9/P

9 780813 056418